# GACE

## Family and Consumer Science Education Practice Questions

Mometrix
TEST PREPARATION

# DEAR FUTURE EXAM SUCCESS STORY

First of all, **THANK YOU** for purchasing Mometrix study materials!

Second, congratulations! You are one of the few determined test-takers who are committed to doing whatever it takes to excel on your exam. **You have come to the right place.** We developed these practice tests with one goal in mind: to deliver you the best possible approximation of the questions you will see on test day.

Standardized testing is one of the biggest obstacles on your road to success, which only increases the importance of doing well in the high-pressure, high-stakes environment of test day. Your results on this test could have a significant impact on your future, and these practice tests will give you the repetitions you need to build your familiarity and confidence with the test content and format to help you achieve your full potential on test day.

**Your success is our success**

**We would love to hear from you!** If you would like to share the story of your exam success or if you have any questions or comments in regard to our products, please contact us at **800-673-8175** or **support@mometrix.com**.

Thanks again for your business and we wish you continued success!

Sincerely,
The Mometrix Test Preparation Team

# TABLE OF CONTENTS

# Practice Test #1

**1. Which of these dairy foods has the most calcium?**

a. A 4.2-oz. slice of fruit cheesecake
b. A 5.3-oz. serving of low-fat yogurt
c. A 1.4-oz. chunk of cheddar cheese
d. A 2.6-oz. serving of plain ice cream

**2. Currently, US laws mandate Nutrition Facts panels on food packaging for:**

a. All foods being sold
b. Most foods but not all of them
c. Foods making nutritional or health claims
d. No foods; it is recommended but not mandatory

**3. With perpetual inventory:**

a. a physical count is done each week.
b. the running count is continually updated.
c. the maximum level is maintained at all times.
d. orders are placed only when the minimum is reached.

**4. Which of the following is best for consumers to do when they want to buy a house?**

a. Look at homes in the location(s) they prefer the most.
b. Let a realtor suggest properties based on their needs.
c. They may do one or all of these things as they choose.
d. Look at listings for homes with prices they can afford.

**5. Borrowers with a poor credit rating will not be eligible for a bank's:**

a. Prime rate
b. Savings deposits
c. Demand deposits
d. Deposit insurance

**6. According to Freud, a boy must do which of these in early childhood to enable him thereafter to have healthy interpersonal relationships?**

a. Not have an Oedipal conflict
b. Resolve the Oedipal conflict
c. Maintain an Oedipal conflict
d. Experience Oedipal conflict

**7. Which of these is most realistic about analyzing financial values and developing financial goals?**

a. Other people cannot recommend any financial goals for an individual.
b. Other people should advise an individual of goals and which to pursue.
c. Individuals must decide for themselves which financial goals to pursue.
d. Financial goals should include saving and investing but never spending.

**8. During which life stage is it most typical to focus on developmental tasks like thinking abstractly, attaining peer group membership, and experiencing sexual relationships?**

a. Early adolescence
b. Later adolescence
c. Middle school age
d. In early adulthood

**9. According to models of developmental tasks at various life stages, when is an adult most likely to develop a perspective related to death?**

a. Around age 22–34
b. Around age 34–60
c. Around age 60–75
d. Around 75–death

**10. According to the AAFCS Code of Ethics Statement of Principles of Professional Practice, AAFCS members do not claim to have expertise in areas wherein they are not educated, trained, and experienced. To which of the following principle categories does this relate?**

a. Integrity and Confidentiality
b. Professional Competence
c. Respect for Diversity
d. Conflict of Interest

**11. In the interior design of a family home, what is true about the placement of windows?**

a. Windows can give good views but no practical benefits.
b. Windows have a tendency to make homes look smaller.
c. Windows are good regardless of number and positions.
d. Windows can create relationships with nature outdoors.

**12. What can cause some kinds of dough to become tough?**

a. Overhandling any fat-based pastry or cookie dough
b. Pinching buttery pastry edges with warm fingers
c. Overhandling candy clay made using chocolate
d. Putting very wet filling into a pie crust dough

**13. An adult has two identically sized and shaped containers holding identical amounts of liquid. S/he pours the same amount from each container into a short, wide glass and a tall, thin glass as a seven-year-old watches. The adult asks the child which glass holds more. The child answers, "They both hold the same amount; I just saw you pour the same amount into each glass." This child demonstrates which ability according to Piaget's theory of cognitive development?**

a. Centration of property
b. Permanence of objects
c. Conservation of volume
d. Egocentrism of thought

**14. Fuzzy fibers that ball up and adhere to the outside of a garment are said to be:**

a. Fuzzing
b. Snagging
c. Breathing
d. Pilling

**15. Which of the following is true regarding development in early childhood?**

a. Young children tend to use speech more than physical aggression during conflict.
b. Young children develop and apply motor skills before verbal skills.
c. Young children often know constructive management of strong emotion.
d. Young children learn social skills directly rather than with puppets.

**16. The prefrontal cortex undergoes significant maturation during which developmental stage?**

a. Early childhood
b. Middle childhood
c. Late childhood
d. Adolescence

**17. What is most accurate about Family and Consumer Sciences in America?**

a. It is a course students are required to take in most high schools.
b. It satisfies the credit in Sciences for graduation in most high schools.
c. It satisfies the Humanities credit for graduation in most high schools.
d. It is a course that is elective for students in most middle schools.

**18. A variety of researchers have found evidence that family recreation provides many benefits, both to families and to individual family members. Which of the following is an example of one of family recreation's benefits to the family as a group?**

a. Teaching moral values and health
b. Improvements in communications
c. Providing educational experiences
d. Fulfilling a diversity among needs

**19. For financial planning, which of the following should an individual or family do first?**

a. Developing what their financial goals will be
b. Identifying alternative actions they will take
c. Evaluating consequences of various actions
d. Determining their current financial situation

**20. When using product or service information to inform consumer decisions, which of these is an example of "soft" information?**

a. Weight
b. Pricing
c. Quality
d. Content

**21. Which of the following vitamins is known to improve the body's ability to use phosphorus and calcium?**

a. Vitamin E
b. Vitamin D
c. Vitamin B-3
d. Vitamin K

**22. Research has found which of the following most often?**

a. Parents are more likely to expect more of their youngest children.
b. Parents are more likely to expect more from their middle children.
c. Parents are more likely to expect the same from all their children.
d. Parents are more likely to expect more of their firstborn children.

**23. Family therapist Virginia Satir identified five common roles of family members. She described only Levelers, who communicate their true feelings honestly, as healthy because their outward communication is congruent with their inward emotions. Which of the other four dysfunctional roles hopes to be loved by being perceived as harmlessly endearing?**

a. Blamers
b. Placators
c. Distractors
d. Computers

**24. Which consumer rights and responsibilities are addressed by the establishment of the Office of Fair Lending and Equal Opportunity under the Dodd-Frank Wall Street Reform and Consumer Protection Act of 2010?**

a. To redress and to choice
b. To redress
c. To be heard
d. To choice

**25. According to Bandura's Social Learning Theory, four conditions are needed for modeling of behaviors to occur. Which of these is most related to having a good reason to imitate another's behavior?**

a. Attention
b. Motivation
c. Retention
d. Reproduction

**26. Which types of fabric are usually most flattering to an overweight body type?**

a. Medium-weight fabrics with a flat texture
b. Soft, fine-gauge knits with a cuddly texture
c. Strong, large-gauge knits with nubby texture
d. Smooth, very shiny fabrics like silk or silk-look

**27. An engineer at an automobile manufacturer discovers a potential issue with the engines of the latest model of cars being produced. The flaw could cause the engine to overheat and catch fire. The engineer brings this issue to the attention of management, but they decide that the likelihood of the engine catching fire is low enough that it does not justify the expense of repairing the cars already produced. However, they agree to adjust the engines on all cars being produced going forward. Which of the following consumer rights is this company failing to meet?**

a. Access to information
b. Marketing transparency
c. Product liability
d. Consumer guarantee

**28. What is the major benefit of vitamin A?**

a. It helps form new cells.
b. It helps protect the body from disease.
c. It can increase a person's concentration and alertness.
d. It can give a person healthy hair and skin.

**29. When scaling a standard recipe intended for 100 people to serve 275 people, the conversion factor is:**

a. 1.25.
b. 2.5.
c. 2.75.
d. 1.75.

**30. Regarding nonverbal forms of communicating, which statement is most accurate?**

a. Messages conveyed via nonverbal means are not found as truthful as verbal messages are.
b. The use of humor in speaking is not included among the areas of nonverbal communication.
c. Increasing globalization means that nonverbal communication is more universally the same.
d. Increasing globalization requires more awareness, observation, and sensitivity of speakers.

**31. Which of the following nutrients is commonly associated with an increased risk of hypertension?**

a. Calcium
b. Fiber
c. Vitamin D
d. Sodium

**32. Someone tells a joke to a group of people, and following the punch line is complete silence. To which component of the communication process does this relate most?**

a. Encoding
b. Feedback
c. Decoding
d. Medium

**33. Currency, relevancy, authority, accuracy, and _______ are the key criteria in evaluating health information found online.**

a. Purpose
b. Functionality
c. Potential
d. Source

**34. According to the attachment styles defined by Mary Ainsworth through her Strange Situation experiments, which of these did she observe about separation anxiety in children aged 12–18 months?**

a. Children who have secure attachments show distress when their mothers leave the room.
b. Children with insecure-ambivalent attachment show no distress if mother leaves the room.
c. Children with insecure-avoidant attachment show extreme distress at the mother's leaving.
d. Children with secure attachment show higher separation anxiety than insecure-ambivalent.

**35. Which common foodborne pathogen is often found in ground beef, sprouts, lettuce, berries, and unpasteurized milk?**

a. *Clostridium botulinum.*
b. *Salmonella enteritidis.*
c. Shiga toxin-producing *Escherichia coli* (STEC).
d. *Staphylococcus aureus.*

**36. In which life stage is it most common for adults to redirect their energy to new activities and roles?**

a. The middle adult ages
b. During later adulthood
c. During early adulthood
d. In adulthood's old age

**37. Compared to families of the past, today's families are more often geographically isolated from their relatives at which socioeconomic level?**

a. Lower-middle-class families
b. Upper-middle-class families
c. Middle-class families
d. Lower-class families

**38. Which of the following is most at risk of contamination with anaerobic bacteria?**

a. Canned foods.
b. Frozen foods.
c. Refrigerated foods.
d. Fresh foods.

**39. What is one common problem with silk clothing?**

a. It is easily damaged by the sun.
b. It is very susceptible to abrasions.
c. It has a tendency to wrinkle.
d. It is very flammable.

**40. In which eating disorder is the patient more likely to retain a normal body weight?**

a. Neither of these
b. Both of these
c. Anorexia
d. Bulimia

**41. To a newborn infant, which of Maslow's levels of needs is most important?**

a. Love, belonging
b. Safety, security
c. Self-actualizing
d. Physiological

**42. Which fabrication method, typical of outerwear, involves stitching a liner fabric in between two outer fabrics?**

a. Knitting
b. Stitch-through
c. Quilting
d. Tufting

**43. According to Gesell's stages of development, at which of the following ages are children most cooperative with their parents?**

a. 8 years
b. 6 years
c. 10 years
d. 9 years

**44. What is true about how you can tell if yeast is still active after long-term storage?**

a. There is no way to test yeast, so you should not store it too long.
b. The only way to tell is to use it in a recipe and see what happens.
c. "Quick-rising" yeast can be "proofed" the same as regular yeast.
d. To "proof" regular yeast, add warm water and then wait 10 minutes.

**45. Which of these is most accurate about realtors who help consumers buy homes?**

a. Realtors who represent buyers cannot work on the same contract as the seller's representative.
b. All realtors are responsible for representing both buyers and sellers at times.
c. Some realtors only represent either buyers or sellers, while others are willing to act in both roles.
d. Realtors must represent both the buyer and the seller in most transactions.

**46. What is the primary consideration in real estate financing for home buyers?**

a. Obtaining a mortgage loan despite the cost or terms
b. A loan that has the best terms with a higher cost
c. A loan that costs the least without the best terms
d. A loan that costs the least with the best terms

**47. According to Schaefer's model of parenting along continua across two dimensions, which of these most accurately corresponds with Baumrind's subsequent definition of parenting styles?**

a. Parents high in warmth/low in hostility and high in control/low in autonomy have a permissive style.
b. Parents high in hostility/low in warmth and high in autonomy/low in control have authoritarian style.
c. Parents high in autonomy/low in control and high in hostility/low in warmth have an uninvolved style.
d. Parents high in warmth/low in hostility and high in autonomy/low in control have authoritative style.

**48. Which of the following is an example of a consumer responsibility?**

a. To make one's concerns heard to those who can address the concerns
b. To have one's voice heard about product development and lawmaking
c. To be able to choose among an abundant variety of goods and services
d. To access information that assures the veracity of product statements

**49. A kitchen is 14 feet long and 10 feet wide, but it has an adjoining pantry 4 feet deep and 4 feet wide. What is the gross area of the kitchen?**

a. 24 square feet
b. 32 square feet
c. 140 square feet
d. 156 square feet

**50. Which of the following elements most makes the floor plan of a house effective?**

a. How people move through it
b. How people use the hallways
c. How it looks from standing up
d. How it looks from sitting down

**51. What is correct regarding Freud's and Erikson's theories of development relative to the life span?**

a. Freud's theory does not cover the entire life span, but Erikson's does.
b. Erikson's theory does not cover the entire life span, but Freud's does.
c. Neither Freud nor Erikson covered the entire life span in either theory.
d. Both Freud's and Erikson's theories do encompass the entire life span.

**52. When a parent is widowed or divorced, toddlers may react more to:**

a. Parental coping and changed routines more than parent loss
b. Changes in familiar routines than how the parent copes
c. How that parent copes than changed routines
d. Parent loss than parental coping or changed routines

**53. Which of the following represents the Fibonacci sequence?**

a. 0, 1, 1, 2, 3, 5...
b. 0, 1, 2, 4, 8, 16...
c. 0, 1, 1.5, 2, 2.5...
d. 0, 1, 3, 6, 9, 12...

**54. Which nutrient is not present in high levels in dairy products?**

a. Vitamin B-12
b. Iron
c. Protein
d. Vitamin A

**55. Which term refers to the buying and selling of goods and services via the internet?**

a. B2B
b. E-commerce
c. Online promotion
d. Mobile shopping

**56. Why do realtors usually advise consumers to obtain pre-approval before choosing a home to buy?**

a. To determine how much money they can afford to spend
b. To be able to accomplish all of these through pre-approval
c. To identify which loan programs will meet their needs best
d. To allow time to find lenders and have their credit checked

**57. In which of Erikson's stages does a child first develop awareness of different social roles in the environment?**

a. Trust vs. Mistrust
b. Industry vs. Inferiority
c. Initiative vs. Guilt
d. Identity vs. Role Confusion

**58. Which of the following is currently accurate legally regarding blended families?**

a. Children may not accept their parenting, but stepparents legally become their parents.
b. Stepparents are not legally recognized as parents unless they adopt the spouse's child.
c. If a parent and stepparent get divorced, laws give visitation rights to the ex-stepparent.
d. The law is unclear regarding stepparents, so rights are decided on a case-by-case basis.

**59. When a home construction company advertises new homes as "energy-efficient" or "energy-saving," which of these are the houses most likely to be?**

a. Houses built using building principles and techniques that are more energy-efficient
b. Houses built in the traditional/standard way but fitted with energy-saving appliances
c. Houses built to minimize impacts on the environment, regardless of costs or comfort
d. Houses built to reduce energy used by electronics, which consume the most energy

**60. In describing high-context vs. low-context styles of communication, what do "sender-oriented values" mean?**

a. The speakers do not consider the values of the listeners.
b. The speaker has responsibility for clearly communicating.
c. The speaker lets listeners be responsible to understand.
d. The speaker uses indirect patterns of verbal orientation.

**61. The temperature hazard zone for food products is:**

a. >150 °F.
b. 135-150 °F.
c. 40-140 °F.
d. <41 °F.

**62. Which of the following foods can be cut and used after mold develops on the food?**

a. Cucumbers.
b. Onions.
c. Tomatoes.
d. Peaches.

**63. Which of the following is accurate regarding future careers for FCS majors?**

a. Accelerating social change causes stress, reducing need for human services administration.
b. Jobs in wellness, long-term health care administration, and dependent care remain stable.
c. More employment opportunities are now developing in the appliance and food industries.
d. There is currently a decrease in the hotel, motel, travel, tourism, and restaurant industries.

**64. Safety is a primary consideration in choosing toys for children. Experts also advise choosing toys from which children can learn, that keep their attention more than briefly, that do not promote aggression, and that parents will also enjoy playing with and will not find irritating. What else is recommended in choosing toys?**

a. Parents should choose different toys for girls than toys they pick for boys.
b. Social interaction and creativity are equally important for toys to promote.
c. Toys that stimulate one sense at a time rather than several are preferable.
d. Problem-solving supersedes eye-hand coordination in what toys develop.

**65. Which of the following is a *disadvantage* of group decision-making?**

a. Group decision-making can reduce cognitive biases.
b. Group decision-making combines skills and abilities.
c. Group decision-making always prevents agreement.
d. Group decision-making work can lead to groupthink.

**66. Creating a list of things to do is less necessary:**

a. When children are teething
b. When both parents work in the home
c. When a daily routine has been established
d. When children are in school

**67. Which of the following vitamins is water-soluble?**

a. Vitamin D
b. Vitamin E
c. Vitamin A
d. Vitamin C

**68. Which vitamins are water-soluble, making them less likely to accumulate to toxic levels in the body?**

a. Just vitamin C
b. All B vitamins
c. None of these
d. All of these are

**69. During which life stage do children cognitively develop an understanding of basic cause-and-effect and object categorization are developmental tasks?**

a. 2 to 4 years
b. 4 to 6 years
c. Birth to 2 years
d. 6 to 12 years

**70. A consumer's credit score is usually a factor in all but which of the following transactions?**

a. Buying a car
b. Buying a home
c. Getting a personal loan
d. Opening a bank account

**71. Among the following cognitive biases to which management is subject, which one is caused by making a decision based on an incorrect generalization from an isolated instance or a sample that is too small?**

a. Prior hypothesis bias
b. Illusion of control bias
c. Representativeness bias
d. Escalating commitment bias

**72. In prioritizing as a time management technique, in which order should tasks be done?**

a. Urgent tasks first, then the important tasks next
b. Important tasks first, then the urgent tasks next
c. Urgent important tasks first, then the important tasks next
d. First the urgent tasks, then the urgent important tasks next

**73. In abusive relationships, which of these is most commonly the case?**

a. When an abuser apologizes and acts normal, he or she is genuinely sorry and intends to try to change.
b. When an abuser apologizes and acts normal, he or she is manipulating the victim and will abuse again.
c. When an abuser apologizes rather than blaming the victim, this is a sign the victim can believe it.
d. When an abuser apologizes rather than blaming the victim, he or she is unlikely to repeat the abuse.

**74. In fabric that is woven using a triaxial weave, what is the third set of yarn called?**

a. The warp
b. The weft
c. The whug
d. The woof

**75. According to Diana Baumrind's theory of parenting styles, which style is considered the ideal?**

a. Permissive
b. Authoritarian
c. Authoritative
d. Uninvolved

**76. Which of the following is *most* accurate regarding freeze-dried cheese?**

a. Freeze-dried cheese costs more than fresh cheese does.
b. Freeze-dried cheese is less expensive than fresh cheese.
c. Experts advise replacing fresh cheeses with freeze-dried.
d. No reconstituting method makes it function like fresh cheese.

**77. In a home designed for a family, which rooms should be farthest apart from each other?**

a. Master bedroom and playroom
b. The kitchen and the family room
c. The family room and dining room
d. Master bedroom and other bedrooms

**78. According to Erikson, which stage of social behavior is most typical of children around 2–3 years old?**

a. Developing control over their physical skills
b. Developing control over their environment
c. Developing trust in parents' meeting needs
d. Developing friendships and success at tasks

**79. Which of the following disorders *always* involves bingeing and purging by definition?**

a. Neither one
b. Anorexia
c. Bulimia
d. Both

**80. What is true about the USDA's Food Pyramid?**

a. MyPlate was replaced by the New Pyramid by the USDA in 2026.
b. MyPlate is the current government food group symbol.
c. New Pyramid and MyPlate do not have the same food groups.
d. New Pyramid had fewer food groups than MyPlate includes.

**81. Which of the following is most consistent with expert advice for healthy eating?**

a. Tracking eating patterns causes obsession and compulsion.
b. Exercising is a better way to alleviate boredom than eating is.
c. An effective way to decrease food intake is skipping meals.
d. Certain foods that are not healthful should never be eaten.

**82. Things like the way family members communicate with one another, family members' eating habits, and what kinds of friends the different family members have are most related to:**

a. Structure of a family
b. Resources of a family
c. The roles in a family
d. Lifestyles of a family

**83. What do wardrobe experts advise to individuals for cleaning out their closets?**

a. To get rid of anything they have not worn in more than a year
b. To get rid of anything that does not fit them and keep the rest
c. To get rid of anything and everything meeting any of these criteria
d. To get rid of anything that is not suited to their personal styles

**84. The Hazard Analysis Critical Control Point (HACCP) management system for food safety addresses the analysis and control of what types of hazards?**

a. Bacterial, fungal, and viral.
b. Organic and inorganic.
c. Biological, chemical, and physical.
d. Animal, insect, and chemical.

**85. When should a home buyer get warranty and insurance coverage for the home?**

a. After closing before moving in
b. When making a bid on a house
c. At the closing of the home sale
d. When applying for a mortgage

**86. Of the following, which is generally the most flattering cut and line to wear for a woman with full hips and thin legs?**

a. A circle skirt
b. A pencil skirt
c. A fishtail skirt
d. An A-line skirt

**87. Which of the following fabric care symbols on a garment means it should be dry cleaned?**

a. A triangle shape
b. A circular shape
c. A square shape
d. A circle in a square

**88. Freezer equipment must be maintained at a temperature of:**

a. 0 °F or below.
b. 5 °F or below.
c. 7 °F or below.
d. 9 °F or below.

**89. Which of the following is true about finding childcare services?**

a. Family-run day cares and traditional facilities charge about the same.
b. Websites like SitterCity.com often charge more than nanny agencies.
c. Compatibility between families is the only caveat with nanny-sharing.
d. Babysitting co-ops are better choices for parents who work part-time.

**90. On which of the following fabrics is it safe to use bleach occasionally?**

a. Spandex
b. Silk
c. Cotton
d. Wool

**91. For trustworthy online sources of quality health information, what is NOT recommended by the FTC?**

a. Websites of federal government agencies
b. Disease-specific nonprofit group websites
c. Search engine results on any health topics
d. Medical school or university websites

**92. Baumrind and other researchers applying her theory of parenting styles have found that children reared by parents with the authoritarian style are most likely to become:**

a. Independent, responsible high achievers
b. Immature, irresponsible, impulse-ridden
c. Obedient, anxious, and moody followers
d. Depressed, low-functioning delinquents

**93. In interpersonal conversations, which main goals entail both the highest cognitive challenge and the highest quality of interaction?**

a. Task goals
b. Identity goals
c. Relationship goals
d. All three of these goals

**94. How did the Morrill Act (1862) further the domestic sciences in America?**

a. By funding industrial colleges with a land grant to teach household management to farm wives
b. By funding industrial colleges with a land grant to teach farm husbands agricultural techniques
c. By funding states with equal land grants for founding agricultural colleges, like with the Turner Plan
d. By funding enforcement of a law banning bigamy and limiting church/nonprofit land ownership

**95. Color analysts often categorize individuals' most flattering color palettes by skin tone into the four seasons. Which of the following represents typically good colors for someone who is a "winter"?**

a. Yellows, oranges, browns, earth tones
b. Blues, greens, purples, black, and white
c. Light, soft pastel tints of all/most colors
d. Bright, vibrant primary/secondary hues

**96. A child whose developmental tasks include learning to play in groups, to identify as a female or male, and to have a basic understanding of right and wrong is typically in which life stage?**

a. The toddler years
b. Early school years
c. Middle school age
d. Birth to two years

**97. The most common type of institutional menu is the:**

a. cycle menu.
b. fixed menu.
c. single-use menu.
d. selective.

**98. Which of the following statements about stain removal is true?**

a. Stained garments can be safely ironed.
b. A fresh stain can be cleaned with bar soap.
c. Milk stains should be treated with hot water.
d. Stained clothing should be cleaned within 24 hours.

**99. Sodium and chloride are major minerals; every day, a person should consume more than ____________ of each.**

a. 100 milligrams
b. 1 kilogram
c. 10 milligrams
d. 10 grams

**100. How do banks and lenders use credit scores to determine creditworthiness?**

a. They show how much money the consumer has available to cover the risk
b. They provide recent historical data of the consumer's use of credit
c. It is an insurance policy if the consumer defaults on a debt
d. They document the consumer's use of credit over the span of their lifetime

# Answer Key and Explanations for Test #1

**1. C:** A 1.4-oz. (40-gram) chunk of cheddar cheese has 296 mg of calcium. A 4.2-oz. (120-gram) slice of fruit cheesecake has 94 mg of calcium. A 5.3-oz. (150-gram) serving of plain low-fat yogurt has 243 mg of calcium. A 2.6-oz. (75-gram) serving of plain vanilla ice cream has 75 mg of calcium. So, the yogurt is second to the cheddar cheese, the cheesecake is third, and the ice cream is fourth.

**2. B:** At present, the FDA and USDA mandate that food packaging contain Nutrition Facts panels for most, but not all foods being sold (B). For example, single-ingredient packages of raw meats and poultry are not presently required to have Nutrition Facts panels on their labels, though the USDA has proposed this requirement before and has recently proposed it again. Foods containing nutritional or health claims (C) on their labels are included among those required to provide Nutrition Facts panels. Nutrition Facts panels are mandatory for most foods; hence (D) is incorrect.

**3. B:** With perpetual inventory, a running count is continually updated. Perpetual inventory systems generally use a software program that automatically updates when purchase units arrive and when issue units are removed, so that the status of the inventory can be assessed at any time and purchase orders can be sent. With this inventory system, physical inventories are not necessary but should be done periodically to ensure that there are no discrepancies or unaccounted-for shrinkage.

**4. C:** Some home buyers prefer to look at listings of homes based on their locations (A); some want to look at listings based on their prices (D); some look at listings based on both their location and pricing criteria; some would rather have a local realtor suggest properties to them according to criteria they have communicated to the realtor (B); and many consumers like to combine these methods to maximize the number of potential properties they can consider. Which approach(es) they choose to look for a home is really up to the consumer.

**5. A:** Borrowers with a poor credit rating will not be eligible for a bank's prime rate. The prime rate is the lowest rate of interest offered by a commercial bank or other lending institution. It is made available only to borrowers with pristine credit ratings since these people and businesses are most likely to repay the loan according to the agreed-upon schedule. Savings deposits, demand deposits, and certificates of deposit are all investitures made by the consumer in a bank; therefore, they do not depend on credit rating. A savings deposit can be withdrawn at any time, while a certificate of deposit must be kept in the bank for a prescribed length of time. A demand deposit is essentially the same thing as a checking account, as the funds within it can be withdrawn at any time and in any amount. Banks are required to have deposit insurance to guarantee that they will be able to return the funds invested by customers.

**6. B:** Freud proposed that like ancient Greek tragedian Sophocles's character Oedipus, who unwittingly murdered his father and married his mother, all boys experience a conflict in early childhood (often around ages 4 to 5) wherein they unconsciously desire their mothers and wish to eliminate their fathers as rivals for the mothers' affection. According to Freud, it was impossible for a boy not to have this conflict (A). He said that young boys resolve this conflict through "identification with the aggressor," i.e. wanting to be like the father and imitating him, thereby relieving guilt over their unacceptable sexual and aggressive impulses toward each respective parent. Perpetuating the conflict (C) was not a solution to Freud but rather an unhealthy fixation that would undermine all relationships. Simply experiencing the conflict (D) was not sufficient in Freud's theory; it must also be successfully resolved.

**7. C:** It can help for other people to recommend financial goals (A), especially for young people about to graduate from high school or college or starting jobs. However, though others can give advice about goals, they should not tell the individual which ones to pursue (B); this is something the individuals must decide for themselves. Financial goals can include savings, investments, and spending as well (D). If someone has a goal to buy a house, car, business, etc., these are included as financial goals, so spending can be as much a part of a person's financial goals as saving or investing to provide for financial security and freedom in the future.

**8. A:** The developmental tasks named are characteristic of early adolescence, around the ages of 12 to 18 years old. Typical developmental tasks in later adolescence (B) include establishing one's sex role identity, becoming independent of one's parents, developing an internalized moral sense, and making career choices. Typical developmental tasks at middle school age (C), around six to 12 years old, include forming and maintaining friendships; performing concrete mental operations; learning academic and social skills; self-evaluation; and engaging in team play. Typical developmental tasks in early adulthood (D) include starting to work at a job, getting married, and having children.

**9. C:** It is more typical for adults to develop a perspective regarding death in later adulthood than in old age when closer to death (D). By old age, they usually have already established a point of view about death and are occupied with reviewing their lives, adjusting to the deaths of spouses, etc. Young adults (A) are typically engaged in other developmental tasks like marrying, starting families, and working. Middle-aged adults (B) are typically involved in tasks like developing their marriages, households, and careers and parenting their children.

**10. B:** In the AAFCS Code of Ethics, in its Statement of Principles of Professional Practice, the category of Professional Competence includes the principle that "AAFCS members claim competence in area(s) for which they have education, training, and experience." The only concept that overlaps across the principles of Integrity and Confidentiality (A) and Conflict of Interest (D) is that of avoiding exploitation. Respect for Diversity (C) does not involve claims of competence but rather having respect for and supporting differences among people's beliefs, backgrounds, and cultures.

**11. D:** Windows in a home can form connections to the natural environment outdoors, which also improve home experiences indoors. In addition to beautiful views when they are in the right places, windows also yield practical benefits (A) by letting in natural sunlight and fresh air. By letting in light and allowing people to see out, windows create the perception that rooms and houses look bigger, not smaller (B). However, architectural designers also need to consider factors like whether a window opens on an unattractive view, interferes with homeowners' privacy, faces in a direction that does or does not let in light at the wrong time(s) of day, etc. Therefore, they must know how many windows to include and where to place them most appropriately (C) to achieve the best effects.

**12. A:** Any fat-based dough, e.g., for pie crusts, scones, cookies, or pastries, will become tough if handled too much. When making filled pastries using a buttery (fat-based) pastry dough, pinching the edges together with warm fingers (B) can make the dough too soft rather than tough. (A solution is to chill the dough first and handle it through a piece of plastic wrap.) Overhandling candy clay made with chocolate (C) will make it soften and melt rather than become tough. Putting very wet filling into pie crust (D) will make the dough soggy rather than tough, especially if the pie plate was not buttered or the dough was not brushed with egg white first.

**13. C:** This child demonstrates conservation of (liquid) volume by knowing both glasses hold the same amount regardless of their shapes or sizes. Centration of property (A) is what a younger child does in focusing on only one property at a time, e.g. either the height or width of the container but not both. Piaget said centration prevents conservation. Object permanence (B) is the realization babies develop that things still exist even when they cannot see them. Egocentrism (D) is characteristic of the thinking of children in the Preoperational stage, when they cannot see things from another person's perspective but only their own.

**14. D:** When the fuzzy fibers of a fabric ball up and adhere to the outside of the garment, they are said to be pilling. The degree to which a fabric "pills" is one criterion of durability. Fuzzing is the emergence of tiny fibers from a yarn, creating the effect of roughness on the outside of the garment. Snagging occurs when fibers catch and are pulled out of the weave. Breathing is the ability of a loosely woven fabric to allow the passage of air. Light fabrics tend to be better at breathing. Creasing is the creation of permanent folds in the fabric. Oftentimes, pants will be worn with an intentional crease along the front and back of the legs.

**15. B:** Children's motor skills typically develop sooner than their verbal skills. During conflict, young children are more likely to use physical aggression like kicking, biting, hitting, and pushing/shoving to get what they want rather than using speech (A). Young children also often have trouble self-regulation emotion, so teachers must help them learn how to manage their strong emotions constructively (C). Young children do not learn social skills only directly; teachers can help develop their social skills by demonstrating aggressive vs. proactive behaviors using puppets (D), which preschoolers find entertaining as well as concrete representations of emotions they can understand.

**16. D:** Adolescence takes place between ages 13 and 18. During this stage, teenagers undergo significant physical changes and hormonal development. Their prefrontal cortexes—the part of the brain responsible for decision-making and judgement—undergo significant maturation. The prefrontal cortex is one of the last regions of the brain to mature and typically finishes around age 25.

**17. C:** In most American high schools, taking Family and Consumer Sciences (formerly called Home Economics) will satisfy credits in Humanities, not Sciences (B), toward graduation. In most US states, a Family and Consumer Sciences course is required in middle schools rather than being an elective (D). In most US states, it is an elective course for high school students rather than a required course (A).

**18. B:** One of many benefits of family recreation researchers have found is that it improves communication within the family. Teaching moral values and healthy lifestyles (A) is a benefit researchers have found family recreation provides children as individual members of the family; providing children with educational experiences (C) is another. Fulfilling the diverse needs (D) of different family members is more of a challenge to planning and engaging in family recreation that researchers have found, rather than a benefit of family recreation to either the family group or individual family members. (Of course meeting the needs of all family members would be a benefit of family recreation when this is actually accomplished; however, researchers have not identified it as a benefit but a challenge, because it is so difficult to achieve with no existing universal structure for programming family recreation.)

**19. D:** The first step in financial planning is to determine what the individual's or family's current financial circumstances are. The second step is to develop what their financial goals will be (A). The third step is to identify different possible actions they may take (B). The fourth step is to evaluate the potential consequences of taking any of those actions among the alternatives (C). Additional steps include making a financial plan of action, implementing it, reevaluating that plan, and changing it as needed.

**20. C:** The quality of a product or service—or how useful it is, how durable, etc.—is classified as soft information, which individual consumers vary in judging. In other words, soft information is subjective. Hard information is objective because it is made up of facts. For example, the weight (A) of a product, the price (B) of a product or service, or the contents (D) of a product (e.g., the ingredients in food, cosmetic, or cleaning products) are all facts and hence are examples of hard information.

**21. B:** Vitamin D is known to help the body absorb the phosphorus and calcium obtained through a person's diet. It is present in small amounts in foods like fish and eggs and is especially present in cod liver oil. Vitamin E is a major antioxidant, meaning that it protects the cells from free radical damage. This vitamin is found in good amounts in wheat germ oil, milk, and plant leaves. Vitamin B-3, also known as niacin, helps to reduce levels of cholesterol in the blood. It is found in yeast, dairy products, and wheat germ. Vitamin K promotes blood clotting. It is abundant in spinach, cabbage, and soybeans. Vitamin A contributes to the growth and maintenance of body tissues. It is particularly present in eggs, spinach, and liver.

**22. D:** Research studies have consistently found that parents are more likely to expect more from their firstborn children. New parents with no previous experience of having their own children are likely to place higher expectations on their first child. By the time they have had more children and experience, they are likely to lower their expectations of their middle (B) and youngest (A) children to be more realistic. Hence, most parents are not likely to have the same expectations of all their children (C).

**23. C:** Distractors are described by Satir as those members who divert the others' attention from problematic issues and the attendant emotions by engaging in various attention-getting behaviors. Distractors may be the "babies" of their families and feel the others will only love them if perceiving them as harmless and cute. Blamers (A) hide their insecurities by attacking the others. Placators (B) try to appease the others to avoid the rejection or disapproval they fear. Computers (D) avoid confronting or expressing feelings by denying all emotion and limiting their communication to only intellectual, objective, or factual topics.

**24. A:** The Dodd-Frank Wall Street Reform and Consumer Protection Act of 2010, among other provisions, established the Office of Fair Lending and Equal Opportunity. The establishment of this office addresses the consumer's rights and responsibilities to redress (B), i.e., the right to request money or other benefits to compensate for a mistake made by a company and the responsibility to seek such compensation; and to choice (D), i.e., the right to a broad range of goods and services available at fair prices; and the responsibility to exercise care in choosing among these. Consumer rights and responsibilities to be heard (C) are addressed by protections for whistleblowers provided by the Consumer Financial Protection Bureau, also established under the Dodd-Frank Wall Street Reform and Consumer Protection Act of 2010.

**25. B:** Bandura said that in order for modeling of behaviors to be effective, the four conditions of attention, retention, reproduction, and motivation were necessary. Attention (A) requires the observational learner to attend to the behavior modeled. Degrees of attention are affected by multiple variables like the functional value of the behavior; its complexity, distinctiveness, prevalence, and affective valence (how emotionally attractive the observer finds it); and the observer's level of arousal, sensory capacities, perceptual set, and having received past reinforcement for similar behaviors and/or for observing others' behaviors. Motivation (B) is most related to the observers' having good reason(s) for observing and imitating others' behaviors, e.g., previous rewards, imagined or promised rewards, and vicarious; i.e., observing others being rewarded for behaviors. Retention (C) involves being able to remember the behaviors one observed. Reproduction (D) involves imitating or replicating the observed behavior.

**26. A:** A medium-weight fabric with just enough stiffness to skim over the body rather than cling to it (but not so stiff as to look boxy) and a flat texture that does not make body parts look bigger is generally most flattering to overweight body types. Soft, fine-gauge knits (B) have a nice cuddly feel, but they cling to the body, showing off every lump and bump, so they are not as flattering to the overweight. Knits of larger gauge yarn with nubby textures (C) make a large body look even larger. Smooth, very shiny fabrics like silk or silky-looking synthetics (D) reflect the light, again making big bodies look bigger; and they may also be clingy.

**27. C:** The automobile manufacturer failed to meet consumer rights regarding liability. If any of the engines catch fire, the manufacturer is liable for any injuries resulting from the fire and also any damage to the vehicle. Consumers have the right to rely on the products they purchase to meet minimum safety standards.

**28. D:** The major benefit of vitamin A is that it helps the body produce healthy hair and skin. Carrots, pumpkins, fish, and eggs are all good sources of vitamin A. Help with forming new cells is a major benefit of folate, or folic acid. There is a great deal of folate in spinach and fortified grains. Vitamin C is one of the primary disease-fighting nutrients. It is obtained most effectively from citrus fruits and broccoli. Concentration and alertness are improved by vitamin B-12. It is most abundant in fish, poultry, and eggs. Calcium is a mineral that helps muscles contract. It is abundant in dairy products and sardines.

**29. C:** When scaling a standard recipe intended for 100 people to serve 275 people, the conversion factor is 2.75.

- Formula: New yield/original yield = conversion factor
- 275/100 = 2.75

The conversion factor is then applied to every ingredient in the standard recipe. For example, if the original recipe called for 2 pounds of carrots, 2 × 2.75 = 5.5 pounds. The time needed for preparation may need to be increased as well as the time needed for cooking.

**30. D:** While increasing globalization means that cultures are mixing and communicating more, this does not mean that nonverbal forms of communication have become more universally similar (C). It means rather that people are exposed to more culturally dissimilar forms of nonverbal communication, requiring speakers to become more aware, observant, and sensitive to these cultural differences. People generally assume nonverbal communication to be more truthful than verbal communication, not vice versa (A). Humor *is* classified among the areas of nonverbal communication (B), as are areas like paralinguistics, proxemics, gestures, posture, body language, facial expressions, eye contact, etc.

**31. D:** A significant portion of American adults consume more sodium (D) than is recommended. This has been associated with an increase in the number of adults who develop hypertension, or high blood pressure, which can threaten an individual's cardiovascular health. Many American adults consume less than the recommended amount of calcium (A), fiber (B), and vitamin D (C). Deficiencies in these nutrients can lead to health complications, but overconsumption of sodium is most closely associated with hypertension.

**32. B:** Four components of the communication process are encoding (A), wherein the sender converts information into symbols representing the ideas involved; the medium (D) whereby the sender transmits the message, e.g., visual, oral, or written; decoding (C), whereby the receiver(s) will interpret the message received in terms of the receiver(s)'s own experiences to gain meaning from the symbols sent (and correct interpretation equals successful communication); and feedback (B), whereby the receiver(s) responds to the sender's message. Feedback includes the receiver's saying something in return, including asking a question, making a facial expression or gesture, writing a message, taking some physical action, or not saying or doing anything. As in this example, even silence is a type of response. In this case, the fact that the receivers did not laugh (or groan, as at a bad pun) indicates that either they did not think the joke was funny or they did not understand it.

**33. A:** Purpose is the fifth criterion in evaluating the validity of an online health resource. This addresses the reason the information exists or has been published. The purpose of reliable health-related information should be to inform the reader. Currency addresses how recent or up-to-date the information is, relevancy addresses the relationship between the information and the user's needs, authority addresses the information's author or publishing organization, and accuracy addresses how reliable or true the information is.

**34. A:** Ainsworth found in her experiments that children with secure attachments to their mothers showed distress when their mothers left the room. She expanded the work of John Bowlby, who defined separation anxiety as a characteristic of normal attachment. Ainsworth found that children she identified as having insecure-ambivalent attachment showed more extreme distress at their mothers leaving than securely attached children, rather than showing no distress (B). However, she found that children she defined with insecure-avoidant attachment showed no distress upon their mothers' leaving the room, rather than showing extreme distress (C). Therefore, children with secure attachment show normal separation anxiety, but this is a lower level of separation anxiety than the level displayed by children with insecure-ambivalent attachment, not higher (D).

**35. C:** STEC is often found in ground beef, sprouts, lettuce, berries, and unpasteurized milk. STEC, especially O157:H7, has been responsible for numerous outbreaks of foodborne disease in the United States. *E. coli* is a common bacterium in the gastrointestinal tract of humans and animals, and most outbreaks are traced to contamination of foodstuffs with animal feces. Solid cuts of meats, such as roasts, chops, and steaks, pose less risk than ground meat because surface contamination is usually destroyed by heat during cooking.

**36. B:** In later adulthood, e.g., around 60 to 75 years, it is a common developmental task to redirect one's energies to new activities and roles as life circumstances change. Common developmental tasks in middle adulthood (A), e.g., around ages between 34 and 60 years, include nurturing marital relationships, parenting, household management, and career management. Early adulthood (C), e.g., around 22 to 34 years old, includes developmental tasks like going to work, getting married, and having children. In old age (D), e.g., from age 75 to death, includes developmental tasks like coping with the physiological changes aging causes, making life reviews, and developing psychohistorical perspectives.

**37. B:** Upper-middle-class families today are more likely to relocate for employment opportunities (e.g., college professors who must move to another university to accept a particular teaching or research position they want and are offered or business professionals whose promotions require relocation, etc.), whereas lower-middle-class families (A), middle-class families (C), and lower-class families (D) are more likely to reside in places where some of their relatives live; and if they move, are more likely to move to other places where they also have relatives living.

**38. A:** Canned foods are at risk of contamination with anaerobic bacteria, which grow in the absence of oxygen, especially if the cans are dented or rusted, so any damaged cans should be discarded, and canned contents should be examined for color and odor before use. Anaerobic bacteria may also grow in modified atmosphere packaged products, in the center of large quantities of stored food where air does not circulate, or in improperly processed foods that are stored at room temperature.

**39. A:** One common problem with silk clothing is that it is easily damaged by the sun. Silken garments can fade quickly if they are not kept out of direct sunlight. For this reason, silk should be kept in a drawer or dark closet. The other answer choices are false statements. Silk is very resistant to abrasions and wrinkles, and it burns very slowly. Silk is renowned for its smoothness. It is considered one of the least coarse fabrics in the world.

**40. D:** In bulimia, the patient binge-eats abnormal amounts of food and then purges by vomiting, and he or she may also abuse laxatives and/or diuretics. In anorexia (C), the patient starves, eating nothing or very little; and some anorexics also vomit and/or abuse laxatives and/or diuretics. However, bulimics typically eat more normal amounts of food outside of their secret binge-eating and purging sessions, so they usually retain more normal body weights and appearances (though they suffer electrolyte imbalances, erosion of the teeth's enamel, and other serious results of all the vomiting). In contrast, anorexics typically become severely underweight and appear emaciated as the disorder progresses because they never eat normal amounts of food.

**41. D:** The most basic level of needs is physiological—for water, sleep, food, elimination, etc.—and comes first in Maslow's hierarchy. These are the needs most important to a newborn infant. Maslow's second level of needs is of those for safety and security (B), which become more important to toddlers. His third level is of needs for love and belonging (A), which become important as children grow. As they get older, they also have needs on Maslow's fourth level, self-esteem, i.e., respect, self-confidence, and achievement. His fifth and most evolved level is of needs for self-actualization (C), which includes problem-solving, creativity, moral and ethical development, accepting the truth, and realizing one's greatest potentials. (Note: Maslow's needs levels do not depend only on age; adults may experience any level as a priority at any time in life. However, infants are not yet cognitively developed enough to be concerned with the higher levels.)

**42. C:** Quilting is the fabrication method of stitching a liner fabric between two outer fabrics. Because this process essentially creates a three-layered fabric, it is used in outerwear and clothing that is meant for cold weather. Knitting is the use of hooked needles to loop yarn threads together. Fabrics made by knitting tend to be very flexible. In stitch-through, a web of fiber is stitched together by a chain of smaller stitches. This technique is also known as malimo. Tufting is a process in which a woven backing has yarns inserted into it, where they are sealed in place with glue. This process, commonly used in the manufacture of carpets, is occasionally used in apparel as well. Finally, weaving is the creation of a network of two yarns, interconnected at right angles throughout the fabric.

**43. C:** Gesell described 10-year-old children as viewing their parents' word as law and wholeheartedly accepting their parents without reservations. He described 8-year-olds (A) as demanding an understanding and close relationship with parents, particularly their mothers. He described 6-year-olds (B) as demoting their mothers from the center of their world to taking second place to themselves, as they now want to be the center of their own world at this age and tend to blame their mothers for whatever is wrong at the time. Gesell described 9-year-olds (D) as becoming more interested in friends and their opinions than in family and their opinions, resisting parental direction, and withdrawing from their family circles as much as they can in favor of independence and self-sufficiency.

**44. D:** Regular active dry yeast can be stored 6 months to 1 year on a shelf or more than 1 year in the freezer. After this long, it is possible to test it, so answer choice A is incorrect. It is not necessary to use the yeast in a recipe (B), which could ruin the food if the yeast is no longer active. Instead, regular yeast can be tested or "proofed" by adding 2¼ tsp. or 1 envelope of yeast to ¼ cup of warm water, stirring, and waiting 10 minutes. If the yeast foams to double the water measure or ½ cup, it is still active. "Quick-rising" yeast, however, cannot be proofed this way (C); its fast-rising effect is lost by dissolving it in liquid.

**45. C:** In the real estate business, realtors can either specialize in buying or selling or they can handle both sides of the transaction. It is also not unheard of for a realtor to represent both the buyer and the seller in the same transaction, though this is certainly not required.

**46. D:** The primary consideration in real estate financing for home buyers is to find a mortgage loan that offers them the best terms (B) and costs them the least money (C) rather than simply being able to obtain a mortgage loan (A) at all, as almost anybody who is able and willing to pay high enough interest rates can obtain a mortgage. However, higher interest rates mean more of the consumer's money will go to interest rather than principal, requiring higher monthly payments that do not further reduce the principal balance owed for the property and taking longer to pay off the loan.

**47. C:** Schaefer's dimensions are (1) along a continuum from warmth to hostility, and concurrently (2) along a continuum from autonomy to control. Comparing these to Baumrind's parenting styles, low control and low warmth equates to her Uninvolved style. Parents with Baumrind's Permissive style (A) have Schaefer's high warmth, but also high autonomy, not low. Parents with Baumrind's Authoritarian style (B) have Schaefer's high hostility, but also high control, not low. Parents with Baumrind's Authoritative style (D) have a balance of Schaefer's dimensions: enough but not excessive (i.e., intrusive, codependent) warmth; sufficient control to set reasonable limits and enforce rules consistently, but not so much to be rigid or overly punitive; enough autonomy to let children make their own decisions and learn from their mistakes, but not so much to leave children without the structure and guidance they need. While high warmth with high control (A) in Schaefer's model does not correlate with a Baumrind parenting style, this combination is often characterized as "smother love."

**48. A:** Making one's concerns heard to those who can address them is an example of the consumer's responsibility for being heard. Having one's voice heard about product development and lawmaking (B) is an example of the consumer's *right* to be heard. Being able to choose among a variety of goods and services (C) is an example of the consumer's *right* to choice. An example of the consumer's *responsibility* for choice is to exercise due care and caution in choosing from among that variety. Accessing information that assures product statements are true (D) is an example of the consumer's *right* to information. An example of the consumer's *responsibility* regarding information is wisely conducting analyses and applications of the available product information.

**49. D:** The gross area of the kitchen is 156 square feet. In interior design, the gross area of a room is its area, as well as the areas of any ancillary spaces. Pantries, closets, and similar spaces are considered ancillary. The area of a room is found by multiplying length by width. Sometimes, the length of a pantry or closet will be referred to as depth. If the shape of a space is irregular (for instance, L-shaped), it is best to divide the room into rectangular spaces, find the areas of these spaces, and then add them together.

**50. A:** The traffic patterns in the floor plan of a house, i.e., how people move through it, are what most make the floor plan work well. Expert home builders say that successful floor plans are not determined by how they look to people when they are standing up (C) or sitting down (D), i.e., when they are still. Instead, they are determined by how easily people can navigate the home when they are moving. Some builders design homes where people go through one room to get to another rather than going through hallways (B), as they find this design makes it easier to see throughout the house and gives the effect of larger rooms.

**51. A:** While Erikson based his theory on Freud's, one major difference between them is that Freud only included stages of development through adolescence, whereas Erikson included stages of development through old age until death. Freud considered the personality to be complete by adolescence, but Erikson viewed it as continuing to develop throughout life.

**52. A:** When a parent is widowed or divorced, younger children can be more likely to feel the effects of changes to their usual routines (B) and of the way that their remaining parent copes with the loss (C) than of the death or departure of one parent, rather than vice versa (D). Toddlers may fear losing the other parent as well, so that parent must give them plenty of reassurance and feelings of security.

**53. A:** The Fibonacci sequence, in which each successive number is the sum of the two previous numbers, begins 0, 1, 1, 2, 3, 5. The Fibonacci sequence is one of the classic proportions used frequently in interior design. It occurs often in nature and has been found to be pleasing to the eye. The quantities of the Fibonacci sequence may be numbers of units or distances.

**54. B:** Dairy products do not contain significant amounts of iron. The other answer choices, however, are nutrients that are abundant in dairy products. Riboflavin is another nutrient found in great quantities in dairy products. According to the USDA, people should eat two or three servings of dairy every day. A serving is equivalent to one cup of milk, three-fourths a cup of yogurt, or one ounce of cheese. People should be careful about which dairy products they consume, as many contain a great deal of fat.

**55. B:** E-commerce is the recognizable term referring to online buying and selling. Consumers look for sites that are easy to navigate (including the checkout function), have recognizable security features, offer mobile device functionality, and feature promotions or other discounts. Mobile shopping and online promotion refer to e-commerce activities. B2B (business-to-business) is one type of e-commerce.

**56. B:** Realtors usually advise consumers to obtain pre-approval before they decide to bid on a particular house for several reasons. For example, through the pre-approval process, consumers can meet in person or online with different lenders and learn about various loan options; this helps them discover how much money they can afford to spend (A) and which loan programs will meet their needs best (C). Another reason that realtors suggest obtaining pre-approval is because purchase forms for real estate commonly stipulate that the buyer applies for financing within 7 to 10 days or some other limited period of time. It can be difficult to locate a lender and undergo a credit check that quickly, and the time pressure can cause consumers to make poor financing decisions. However, if they have found loan officers and loan programs ahead of time, it is much easier to make a well-informed decision and complete a financing application within the time limit.

**57. C:** Erikson's stage of Initiative vs. Guilt occurs during the preschool years of early childhood when children begin exploring their environments, first develop awareness of the different social roles existing around them, and experience feelings of either purpose and accomplishment or guilt and inhibition. Erikson identified the family as the primary influence on children's development during this stage. Trust vs. Mistrust (A) occurs during infancy when a baby's needs are either met fully and consistently, engendering feelings that the world can be trusted; or incompletely and/or inconsistently, fostering a general mistrust of people. Industry vs. Inferiority (B) occurs when children start school, their world widens from the family to school and social relationships, and they develop a sense of either mastery or inadequacy.

**58. B:** Currently, existing laws do not recognize stepparents as parents of the children whose parents they marry. Hence, in order to have legal parental rights to their new spouses' children, stepparents must legally adopt those children. If a parent and stepparent get divorced (and the stepparent has not adopted to gain legal parental status), the law does not grant any visitation rights to the ex-stepparent (C). Current US law uniformly does not recognize stepparents as legal parents. Thus, it is not true that the law is unclear; and stepparent rights to custody or visitation of ex-stepchildren are not decided case by case (D), but do not legally exist.

**59. A:** Concerns over climate change and protecting the environment have prompted many construction companies to research building science principles to make new houses more energy-efficient. These houses are not built in traditional ways while simply containing energy-saving appliances (B); rather, they reduce the use of energy in the house greatly from the use in a house built, for example, seven years ago. These new houses are built not only to minimize the carbon footprint, i.e., the environmental impact, of those living in them; they are also built to cost homeowners less in energy expenses and to make living there more comfortable for them (C). Building scientists find that heating and cooling are what consume the most energy in houses, not electronics (D).

**60. B:** Sender-oriented values are characteristic of low-context communication, wherein the speaker is responsible for the clarity of his or her communication, rather than the listeners having responsibility for understanding it (C). This does not mean the speaker ignores the values of the listeners (A). In low-context communication, which has sender-oriented values rather than interpreter-sensitive values (where the listener is responsible to understand), the speaker uses direct patterns of verbal orientation rather than indirect patterns (D), which are used in high-context communication.

**61. C:** The temperature hazard zone for food products is 40-140 °F.

| | |
|---|---|
| **Above 140 °F** | Safe temperature to hold hot foods |
| **40-140 °F** | HAZARD ZONE |
| **Below 40 °F** | Safe temperature to hold cold foods—retards bacteria and prolongs shelf life |

When holding hot foods, they should be stirred periodically to redistribute heat and should be covered to prevent heat dissipation and contamination. When holding cold foods, packages should not be stored in direct contact with ice water and unpackaged food should not be stored directly in contact with undrained ice except for whole raw fruits and vegetables and raw fish and chicken received in iced shipping containers.

**62. B:** Onions can be cut and used after mold develops on the food. Mold-affected foods:

- Cut and use: peppers, broccoli, cauliflower, onions, garlic, potatoes, turnips, zucchini, winter squash, apples, pears, cabbage, and hard cheese.
- Discard: Cucumbers, tomatoes, bananas, apricots, peaches, melons, berries, pastries, breads, soft cheeses, dairy products (except hard cheese), processed meats, canned foods, peanut butter, juices, and leftovers.

**63. C:** The food and appliance industry currently is seeing increases in the number of jobs available for FCS professionals. The rapidity of social change today increases individual stress throughout the life span; this increases the need for human services administration rather than reducing it (A). Health care jobs, especially long-term care administration, wellness, and dependent care, are not remaining stable (B) but are increasing. Employment opportunities in the hospitality industries, i.e., hotels, motels, and restaurants, and travel and tourism industries are not currently decreasing (D) but expanding as well.

**64. B:** Experts recommend that parents choose toys that stimulate both creativity and social interaction. They advise toys that both boys and girls can play with are better (A), which also saves money for parents with both. Experts recommend toys that stimulate several senses rather than just one at a time (C). Additionally, they find that eye-hand coordination and problem-solving skills are equally important for toys to develop, rather than one over the other (D).

**65. D:** "Groupthink" is a disadvantage of group decision-making that happens when all the members of the group want so much to agree that they may unanimously adhere to the leader's idea, becoming blinded to alternative ideas. Each individual member is convinced by the power of the group as a whole that they must promote the given idea. Groupthink represents decision-making that is biased rather than objective. On the other hand, an advantage of group decision-making is that it can reduce the cognitive biases (A) that often exist more strongly in individually made decisions. Another advantage of group decision-making is that it benefits from the combined skills and abilities (B) of all group members. Always preventing agreement (C) would be a disadvantage of group decision-making if this were true; however, the facts that many management decisions are made in groups and that group think can occur prove that it is not true. Since agreement is often possible in group decision-making, (C) is not a valid disadvantage.

**66. C:** When a daily routine has been established, it is less necessary to create a list of things to do. Making lists is one of the best ways to organize tasks and to keep from being overwhelmed by responsibilities. However, a daily routine makes certain tasks habitual, which can eventually eliminate the need for the list. For instance, a parent might get up every morning and go through the same steps to get his children ready for school. Since this set of tasks is performed habitually, it does not need to be written down. In addition, the development of a routine helps get the body and mind accustomed to performing certain tasks at certain times. Most people find that a routine makes it less difficult for them to find the motivation to perform unpleasant tasks.

**67. D:** Vitamin C is water-soluble, meaning that it is absorbed into the blood stream and can be forced out of the body through urine and sweat. For example, caffeinated beverages can increase the urine stream and thereby diminish the absorption of water-soluble nutrients like vitamin C. Vitamin B is another water-soluble nutrient. Other vitamins, including A, D, E, and K, are absorbed by the intestinal membrane; these vitamins are said to be fat-soluble. Vitamin D can also be obtained from sunlight.

**68. D:** Vitamin C (A) and all of the B-complex (B) vitamins (thiamine, riboflavin, niacin, pantothenic acid, pyridoxine, biotin, folic acid, and cobalamin) are water-soluble, meaning they can be dissolved in water. As such, they are not typically stored in the body's tissues in large amounts; whatever the body cannot absorb is usually excreted in urine and perspiration. Hence, they are unlikely to accumulate to toxic levels in the body (C). (Fat-soluble vitamins are absorbed in fat and can be stored in the body tissues, where they can build up; so unlike with water-soluble vitamins, one can take in excessive fat-soluble vitamins [vitamins A, D, E, and K] that remain in the body.)

**69. C:** Infancy, i.e., birth to 2 years, is a life stage that includes developmental tasks of cognitively understanding simple causality, the nature of objects, and categorization, as well as early emotional development, social attachment, maturation in motor, perceptual, and sensory functions, etc. Toddlerhood (A) includes developmental tasks of self-control, language, elaborated locomotion, pretend play, etc. Early school ages (B) include developmental tasks of group play, gender role identification, early moral development, etc. Middle school ages (D) include tasks of performing concrete mental operations; learning skills; self-evaluation; developing friendships; playing on teams, etc.

**70. D:** A consumer's credit score may be considered when a consumer buys a car or home if the transaction involves a loan, and it will also be considered if an individual applies for a personal loan. However, one's credit score is not usually considered when opening a bank account, as the account holder is depositing money rather than borrowing it.

**71. C:** The cognitive bias based on representativeness occurs when a manager makes a decision based on wrongly generalizing about something that only happened once or about a sample that is too small to be representative of an entire group. The prior hypothesis bias (A) occurs when a manager makes decisions based on beliefs he or she has previously formed about a relationship among factors, even though these beliefs are proven wrong by the evidence. The illusion of control bias (B) occurs when a manager overestimates how much he or she is able to control what will happen. The escalating commitment bias (D) occurs when a manager has already committed significant resources to a project, and then after problems with it are revealed through feedback, commits even more resources to it in an attempt to resolve the problems.

**72. C:** Urgent tasks need immediate attention but are not necessarily important in the long term. Important tasks are significant in the long run; e.g., they help us attain our long-term goals or otherwise have meaningful consequences over time. Tasks that are both urgent and important will both precipitate crises if neglected, and they also yield long-term benefits. Therefore, in prioritizing, one should complete all urgent important tasks first and then concentrate on those tasks that are not urgent but are the most important. One needs to be able to identify whether tasks are urgent, important, or both and to what degree in order to prioritize them in this way.

**73. B:** In abusive relationships, when an abuser apologizes and acts normal, he or she is usually not genuinely sorry and does not intend to change. Abusers may blame the victim for causing the abuse, or they may apologize, which is not a sign the victim can believe him or her. In spite of apologies, the abuser is likely to repeat the abuse.

**74. C:** Woven fabrics can be made using a plain weave, a twill weave, a satin weave, or a triaxial weave. In the plain weave, one yarn alternates going over and under the other. The two yarns at right angles are called the warp (A) and the weft (B). In the twill weave, the weft goes under and over two or more warp yarns at regular intervals. In the satin weave, each yarn goes over four or more others before crossing under another one. The low twist and long "float," or distance yarn goes between crossings, make satin smooth and shiny. In the triaxial weave, yarns go in three directions instead of only two. In addition to a warp and weft, the third yarn direction is called the whug (C). Woof (D) is an older term that can be interchanged with weft.

**75. C:** According to Baumrind, the authoritative parenting style is ideal in its combination of high standards, clear expectations, reasoned discipline, and warmth and nurturance. Authoritative parents give children balanced amounts of independence and guidance, respect and love, and firmness and kindness. The permissive (A) parenting style is very loving and warm, but it is also overly indulgent and lacking in limits, consequences, and control. The authoritarian (B) parenting style is overly controlling and rigid while lacking in warmth. The uninvolved (D) parenting style lacks both warmth and control.

**76. A:** Freeze-dried cheese is a good way to have cheese in long-term storage for emergencies, etc. However, it does cost more than fresh cheese does (B). Food storage experts do not recommend using freeze-dried cheese regularly to replace fresh cheeses (C). Rather, to ensure one's comfort with using it, they recommend trying it in a few of one's favorite recipes. There are two ways to reconstitute freeze-dried cheese. The quicker method—placing it on paper towels, spraying with water, stirring, and waiting—is fine for melting the cheese and using it in recipes. The method that takes longer—drizzling cold water over it in a bowl while stirring continuously and then refrigerating in a zip-lock bag for several hours to overnight before use—rehydrates the cheese to be more like and function like fresh cheese (D).

**77. A:** In a family home, the parents are afforded more privacy if their master bedroom is not too close to a playroom or other parts of the house that tend to be noisy. To enhance togetherness with family members and guests, open floor plans often have kitchens, family rooms (B), and dining rooms (C) flowing together easily to facilitate visiting and preparing and serving meals. While parents and teenagers may like their bedrooms a bit farther apart for privacy, parents typically want their master bedroom closer to younger children's bedrooms (D) so they can more easily hear, see, check on, and get to them.

**78. A:** In Erikson's theory of psychosocial development, infants from birth to around 18 months learn to develop trust or mistrust in parents' meeting their needs (C) fully and consistently or not. Children aged around 2–3 years, engaged in toilet training and asserting their independence, are developing control over their personal physical skills. Preschoolers aged around 3–5 years, exploring the world around them, are developing and asserting their control over the environment (B). Children beginning school around 6 years old are engaged in learning to form new friendships and other social relationships and learning to address the demands of new tasks at school (D).

**79. C:** By definition, bulimia is a disorder wherein the patient binge-eats excessive amounts of food and then purges it by inducing vomiting, abusing laxatives, or both. Anorexia (B), a disorder wherein the patient starves, eating almost no food, and often also exercises excessively, *sometimes* but *not always* also includes binge-eating and purging, or just purging.

**80. A:** Although the "food pyramid" has long been familiar to most Americans (e.g., the USDA's former MyPyramid and also Mediterranean, Asian, and Latin American Diet Pyramids), the USDA launched the New Pyramid in January 2026. Hence the USDA refers to the New Pyramid as the current government food group symbol rather than MyPlate (B). The New Pyramid does have all of the same food groups as MyPlate did (C). Hence, the New Pyramid does not have fewer food groups than MyPlate (D). However, the New Pyramid prioritizes protein more than MyPlate did, and it suggests fewer grains.

**81. B:** One tip from nutrition experts for healthy eating is to exercise instead of eat to relieve boredom. While eating should be interesting and enjoyable, it should be done out of hunger, not boredom. Experts do advise keeping a log or diary of what foods we eat, when we eat them, why, etc. Keeping records does *not* cause obsession or compulsion (A), it is the other way around: people with obsessive-compulsive disorder or prone to obsessive-compulsive tendencies may think obsessively and behave compulsively about anything, including keeping eating records. Keeping track of eating helps most people understand their eating habits and change them if needed. Experts advise *not* skipping meals (C), which can cause unstable blood sugar levels, fatigue, and subsequent overeating. Experts also advise people *not* to prohibit themselves from ever eating certain foods, even those considered unhealthy (D). This encourages abnormal attitudes toward food and bingeing on either the forbidden foods or allowed ones.

**82. D:** Family lifestyle is a factor affecting family relationships that includes such elements as communication styles, eating habits, and kinds of friends of the family members. Family structure (A) includes such examples as single-parent families, blended families with stepparents, two-parent families, and extended families. Family resources (B) include such things as how much money the family has, how much time, how much education, how many friends, social support networks, etc. Family roles (C) encompass both basic roles, such as parent, child, sibling, and grandparent; and other roles family members adopt like troublemaker, peacemaker, clown, disciplinarian, etc.

**83. C:** Wardrobe experts advise individuals to use "tough love" on their closets and get rid of anything they have not worn for more than a year (A), anything that does not fit them (B), or anything that is not consistent with their personal styles (D) rather than only one of these. For those who can afford it, experts recommend that if they cannot bear to part with many such items or have trouble deciding which things to get rid of, they should employ a personal stylist for help.

**84. C:** The HACCP management system for food safety addresses the analysis and control of biological, chemical, and physical hazards. HACCP is used in all segments of the food industry. The seven HACCP principles include:

1. Conduct hazard analysis
2. Determine critical control points
3. Establish critical limits
4. Establish monitoring procedures
5. Establish corrective actions
6. Establish verification procedures
7. Establish record keeping/documentation procedures

**85. C:** Home buyers should get home warranty and insurance coverage at the closing of the sale. Thus, they should consult an insurance broker or a realtor before the closing to get information and make choices. It may violate lender requirements to obtain insurance after the closing (A), but it would be too early when making a bid on a house (B) since the home buyer does not know yet if he or she will end up buying the house when bidding. It would also be premature to obtain insurance when applying for a mortgage (D), which the buyer should do before making an offer for a specific house to the seller.

**86. D:** An A-line skirt is widest at the hem, balancing out full hips without excess fabric to make the figure look bigger. The full profile of a circle skirt (A) can make the hips look even fuller and accentuate the thinness of thin legs below the hem. A pencil skirt (B) has a narrower hem and fits closely overall; this would exaggerate the contrast between full hips and thin legs. A fishtail skirt (C) is very narrow around the knees and then flares out below the knees. While this would disguise skinny legs, it would also magnify full hips.

**87. B:** According to symbols developed by the American Society for Testing and Materials (ASTM) and FTC and adopted and disseminated by the American Cleaning Institute, a circle is the fabric care symbol meaning to dry clean a garment. A triangle (A) indicates a garment can be bleached. A square (C) means to dry the garment, with various added symbols indicating how to dry (e.g., line or hang dry, drip dry, dry flat, dry in shade, etc.). A circle inside of a square (D) indicates tumble drying, on any heat if the circle is clear. If the circle is black, it means tumble dry with no heat. A circle with one dot means low heat; two dots mean medium heat; and three dots mean high heat. Each of these symbols with an "X" over them means respectively NOT to dry clean, bleach, dry, or tumble dry.

**88. A:** Freezer equipment must be maintained at a temperature of 0 °F or below. The refrigerator temperature (40 °F or below) and freezer temperatures should be recorded in the temperature log at least twice daily (AM and PM) and should be signed by the individual taking the measurements. In the case of a power outage such as with a natural disaster, a full freezer will usually hold its temperature for approximately 48 hours and a half-full freezer for 24 hours.

**89. D:** Babysitting co-ops involve several couples forming a group to rotate caring for each other's children. Each earns credits or points for care hours given, redeemed for their own children's care by other members. Additionally, two sets of parents may informally exchange a few care hours weekly with one another. These arrangements are easier for parents working part-time than those working full-time. Parents will find that family-run daycares, operated in providers' homes and often including providers' children, typically charge much less than traditional daycare facilities (A). Searching for childcare on websites costs less than using nanny agencies (B), which can cost thousands in up-front charges, whereas charges on websites like SitterCity.com can offer free memberships. Families not only need compatibility in parenting practices and attitudes for nanny-sharing; an additional caveat (C) is if one family discontinues the service, leaving the other to scramble to locate another family to share or else pay the nanny's entire salary alone.

**90. C:** It is safe to use bleach on cotton if it is done so occasionally. If bleach is frequently applied to cotton or other cellulosic fibers, the fabric may be damaged. Bleach should not be used on any other fabrics, as it has the ability to cause serious damage. Bleach will often dissolve fabrics made of protein-based fibers, such as silk, wool, and cashmere. Although bleach can be a valuable tool for fabric cleaning, it must be used sparingly to avoid irreversible damage to fibers.

**91. C:** For finding trustworthy online sources of reliable, current health information, the Federal Trade Commission (FTC) recommends visiting federal government agency websites (A), like http://www.nlm.nih.gov/medlineplus/, http://healthfinder.gov/, https://www.healthcare.gov/; http://www.cdc.gov/, http://medicare.gov/, www.fda.gov/consumer, http://www.cancer.gov/, www.nia.nih.gov, and http://womenshealth.gov/. Nonprofit groups focusing on specific diseases or conditions also provide reliable websites (B) offering research information and education to the public; these sites typically have .org extensions (though the FTC also warns consumers to beware phony .org sites set up by scammers). Websites run by medical schools and universities (D)—generally ending with .edu—or by reputable health facilities are also good sources. However, as the FTC points out, the results shown from typing any given health topic into a search engine often include unreliable or outdated websites.

**92. C:** Baumrind and other researchers applying her theory of parenting styles have found that the authoritarian style, which features rigid rules and insistence on obedience; a lack of warmth; a tendency to punish children physically, insult them verbally, or withdraw approval or love to coerce them to conform, tends to produce children who are well-behaved but anxious, moody, and more likely to follow than to lead. Independent, responsible, high-achieving children (A) are likely to be the products of the authoritative parenting style. Immature, irresponsible, impulse-ridden (B) children are likely to be the products of the permissive (also called permissive-indulgent) parenting style. Depressed, low-functioning children who tend toward delinquency (D) are likely to be the products of the uninvolved (also called permissive-uninvolved) parenting style.

**93. D:** Task goals (A) involve the official purpose of a conversation, for example, discussing who will be responsible for making decisions on behalf of an aging parent when the parent is no longer capable of doing so. Identity goals (B) involve protecting the identities of both or all parties in the conversation; for example, when family members feel caring and responsible for bringing up the aforementioned subject, while the parent feels able to have continuing autonomy in spite of failing health. Relationship goals (C) involve maintaining interpersonal connections; for example, the closeness of family members in the example given enables their open discussion of a challenging subject. Conversations that present both the greatest cognitive challenge and the highest quality (by combining seeing others' perspectives and accomplishing their own goals) incorporate all three of these goals (D) at the same time.

**94. A:** The Morrill Act funded land grants to US states to create agricultural colleges. This law did enable these colleges to educate farmers in agricultural techniques (B); however, the way it furthered domestic sciences in America specifically was by enabling these same colleges to educate the farmers' wives in household management (A). The Turner Plan, written by Illinois College's Professor Jonathan Baldwin Turner, gave states equal land grants for agricultural colleges. However, the Morrill Act, introduced by Vermont congressman Justin Smith Morrill, did *not* allocate *equal* land grants to all states (C), but grants of variable sizes according to how many congressional representatives and senators each state had. This favored the eastern states, which had larger populations. The Morrill *Anti-Bigamy* Act, also passed in 1862 under President Abraham Lincoln, banned bigamy and limited church/nonprofit land ownership (D), targeting the Utah Territory's Mormons; however, its enforcement was *not* funded; Lincoln never enforced it; and it did not further domestic sciences.

**95. B:** The "winter" palette is composed of cool colors and black and white for neutrals, which flatter the cool, blue-based skin tones of a "winter." Warm, yellow-based earth tones (A) are most flattering for the "autumn" palette of people with warm, yellow-based and olive skin tones. Light, soft pastels (C) are most flattering to the pale, delicate skin tones of "summer" people. Individuals with higher coloring are most flattered by the bright, vibrant colors (D) of the "spring" palette.

**96. B:** Children in the early school years, e.g., from 4 to 6 years old, have developmental tasks including learning to play in groups, identifying with a gender role, and early moral development. Toddlers (A), e.g., from 2 to 4 years old, have developmental tasks including locomotion beyond toddling, symbolic representation and pretend play, developing language, and learning self-control. Children in middle school (C), e.g., from 6 to 12 years old, have developmental tasks including making friends, performing concrete mental operations, learning academic and social skills, participating as a team member in playing games, and evaluating themselves. Infants (D), e.g., from birth to 2 years old, have developmental tasks including motor, perceptual, and sensory maturation; basic emotional development; social attachment; sensorimotor cognition; understanding basic causation, objects, and categorizing.

**97. A:** The most common type of institutional menu is the cycle menu. Types of institutional menus include:

- Cycle: repeating menu over a specified period of time, such as monthly.
- Fixed: the menu remains unchanged from day to day, such as food offered in a cafeteria.
- Single-use: a special menu prepared to be used one time, such as for a celebration.
- Selective: this type of menu allows the individuals to order meals from a number of options before meal service. A selective menu may be based on a fixed or a cycle menu.

**98. D:** Stained clothing should be cleaned within 24 hours; after a day, many stains will have set and will be almost impossible to remove. The other answer choices are false statements about stain removal. It is not a good idea to iron stained objects, as the heat is likely to set the stain. Bar soap should not be used on fresh stains because it too has the capacity to set stains. Hot water can set stains caused by proteins, like blood, milk, and eggs. It is not considered safe to wash clothing with chemical stains alongside regular laundry. Although most washing machines are strong enough to remove toxic chemicals, there is no sense in taking the risk.

**99. A:** A person should consume at least 100 milligrams of major minerals, including sodium and chloride, every day. Of course, sodium and chloride can both be obtained from table salt. Some of the other major minerals are potassium, calcium, phosphorus, and magnesium. Trace minerals, such as iron, zinc, and copper, need only be consumed at a rate of approximately 10 milligrams every day. The precise effect of these minerals on the body has not yet been determined.

**100. B:** A credit score is a numerical representation of a consumer's history with credit. It is based on several factors, including payment history, total debt, length of credit history, types of credit, and new credit. Typically, negative items on a credit report that affect credit scores remain for up to 7 years and are eventually removed. Lenders use the credit score to determine the risk of the consumer defaulting on the loan. The higher the credit score, the more likely a consumer will be approved for lending.

# Practice Test #2

**1. According to some models of family life stages, which stage includes a developmental task of establishing the foundations for a model of family life?**

a. The stage that involves leaving the home
b. The stage of family of origin experiences
c. The stage of becoming a childless couple
d. The stage just prior to becoming married

**2. Which of the following websites would be the LEAST reliable for finding health-related information?**

a. www.health.harvard.edu
b. www.cdc.gov
c. www.mayoclinic.org
d. www.tuftsuniversity.biz

**3. All of the following are reportable diagnoses according to the FDA Food Code EXCEPT:**

a. *Shigella* spp.
b. Shiga-toxin producing *Escherichia coli* (STEC)
c. hepatitis B.
d. *Salmonella* (nontyphoidal).

**4. In interior design, the arrangement of elements in a pattern around some central point is known as:**

a. Symmetrical balance
b. Gradation balance
c. Asymmetrical balance
d. Radial balance

**5. When used for weight management, which component of cognitive-behavioral therapy (CBT) is most reflected in a person's not eating in certain environments?**

a. Positive self-statements
b. Readiness for change
c. Breaking linkages
d. Self-monitoring

**6. When shopping for a car, which of the following should consumers consider most?**

a. The car's appearance
b. The car's brand name
c. The car's performance
d. The car's planned uses

**7. When a couple with children divorces, which family relationship factors often receive direct and/or indirect effects?**

a. The structure of the family and community expectations
b. The income for the family and the structure of the family
c. Community expectations and the income for the family
d. The structure and income of the family and community expectations

**8. Which of the following populations has a lower dietary requirement for iron?**

a. Vegetarians
b. Young children
c. Pregnant women
d. Postmenopausal women

**9. In his attachment theory regarding parents and children, John Bowlby defined four elements of attachment. Which of these did he say enables a young child to explore the environment?**

a. A secure base
b. The safe haven
c. Separation distress
d. Proximity maintenance

**10. When was the Federal Trade Commission (FTC) established?**

a. 1914
b. 1934
c. 1979
d. 1995

**11. In determining one's current financial situation for financial planning, what is true about which elements to include?**

a. For planning purposes, use total income after taxes.
b. Living expenses and debts are really the same thing.
c. When listing assets, including savings is unnecessary.
d. When listing income, use gross income before taxes.

**12. The FCCLA (Family, Career and Community Leaders of America) student organization helps its members to develop personally through Family and Consumer Sciences education and several areas, e.g., character development and creativity. Among four other areas, which is reflected in a student's evaluating several different insurance policies on multiple features and selecting the most suitable one?**

a. Career preparation
b. Critical thinking skill
c. Practical knowledge
d. Interpersonal communication

**13. Which fabric is best for blocking sunlight?**

a. Green satin
b. Black cotton
c. White cotton
d. Black satin

**14. An effective time management plan:**

a. Encourages students to do their most difficult tasks first
b. Eliminates every possible distraction
c. Includes time for meals
d. Eschews lists

**15. To avoid cross contamination, it's important to:**

a. isolate raw foods from prepared/ready-to-eat foods.
b. avoid using commercially washed precut bagged produce.
c. always use commercially washed precut bagged produce.
d. soak all fresh produce in water to clean it.

**16. What is one problem associated with the over-consumption of protein?**

a. Dehydration
b. Increased muscle mass
c. Strained liver and kidneys
d. Heart palpitations

**17. Of the following career information that young people need, which is most likely to help them identify their career interests and preferences?**

a. Exposure to higher education and other lifelong learning opportunities
b. Exposure to information on job opportunities that leads to living wages
c. Training in job-seeking skills and in basic workplace skills ("soft skills")
d. Participating in career assessments and job-based exploration activity

**18. The National Association of Teacher Educators for Family and Consumer Sciences assigned work groups to examine requirements of National Standard 9, Student and Program Assessment, of the National Standards for Teachers of Family and Consumer Sciences. In 2005, these work groups reported four expectations for beginning or pre-service FCS teachers. Which choice accurately reflects one of these expectations?**

a. They should know, but not interpret, standards and criteria for FCS programs and student learning.
b. They should collect data about programs and learning using only normed, standardized assessment.
c. They should both reflect and refer to external evidence but not thereby change teaching practices.
d. They should justify decisions for program design and teaching practices using data-based evidence.

**19. Regarding needs parents must meet for children, which of the following is correct according to the hierarchy of needs Abraham Maslow proposed in his humanistic theory of motivation and personality?**

a. Parents must make children feel they are loved before worrying about their feeding and rest.
b. Enabling children to fulfill their highest potentials in life takes precedence over all other needs.
c. Before they can keep children safe, parents must see they get enough water, food, and sleep.
d. Parents should promote children's self-esteem first and then their family acceptance and love.

**20. In terms of career education, the AAFCS's Education Fundamentals certification can help recipients gain jobs and continuing education in which kinds of careers?**

a. Public school systems but not private schools
b. Corporate businesses and nonprofits equally
c. School systems but not in higher education
d. At schools more than after-school programs

**21. Which of the following would be found on a reliable health product?**

a. The phrase "contains calcium to help build strong bones"
b. The terms "nontoxic" and "all natural"
c. Personal testimonials from consumers
d. The phrase "satisfaction guaranteed"

**22. Learning in the same way as others but at an overall slower rate is MOST descriptive of which developmental disability?**

a. The autism spectrum
b. Intellectual disability
c. Sensory impairment
d. A learning disability

**23. All of the following vegetables are high in vitamin A EXCEPT:**

a. kale.
b. carrots.
c. Brussels sprouts.
d. cauliflower.

**24. During early childhood, children especially need ______ in their diets to support rapid bone growth.**

a. Magnesium
b. Calcium
c. Potassium
d. Starches

**25. A consumer's credit score is directly influenced by which of the following factors?**

a. Debt repayment history
b. Employment history over the last five years
c. Marital status
d. Income level

**26. Research finds consumers are less interested in using price data to inform their health care decisions under which of these conditions?**

a. The consumers incur high out-of-pocket expenses.
b. The consumers like the doctor that they are seeing.
c. The consumers' medical conditions are nonurgent.
d. The consumers have few provider preconceptions.

**27. The USDA recommends that the majority of food in a healthy diet should be:**

a. Proteins and grains
b. Vegetables and protein
c. Grains and dairy food
d. Fruits and vegetables

**28. Which of the following is true about the relationship of gender stereotypes to laws and policies?**

a. Stereotypes are attitudes, but they never attain any legal status.
b. Stereotypes often become laws when legislation supports them.
c. Stereotypes contributing to laws for good intentions do no harm.
d. Stereotypes that influence laws only discriminate against women.

**29. When making a schedule, children should be encouraged to**

I. Include some free time
II. Place the hardest tasks first
III. Block out long stretches for completing all homework

a. I only
b. II only
c. III only
d. I and II

**30. An individual with the developmental disability of cerebral palsy is *most* likely to need special responses and resources addressing which area?**

a. Motor development
b. Cognitive development
c. Emotional development
d. Social skills development

**31. Regarding communication patterns, which of the following is accurate?**

a. High-context communication uses a clear, firmer voice.
b. Low-context communication uses the nonverbal more.
c. Low-context communication has an indirect verbal style.
d. High-context communication is indirect communication.

**32. Which of the following is the most accurate definition of opportunity cost?**

a. What you get from giving up something else
b. What you have to give up to get something
c. An exchange, always measurable as money
d. The dollar price to buy a specific opportunity

**33. A couple married and had children after obtaining college degrees and finding careers in their fields. Which of these factors likely had the greatest impact on this decision?**

a. Environment
b. Personality traits
c. Tolerance
d. Socioeconomics

**34. In Piaget's theory of cognitive development, which stages occur during early childhood, i.e., from birth to the age of eight years?**

a. Sensorimotor, preoperational, concrete operational
b. Preoperational, concrete operational, formal operational
c. Sensorimotor, preoperational, formal operational
d. Trust vs. Mistrust, Iniative vs. Guilt, Industry vs. Inferiority

**35. Among family roles identified by Virginia Satir, which of these is considered healthy and effective?**

a. Blaming others
b. None of these
c. Pleasing others
d. Diverting others

**36. Which special needs are most often characteristic in autism spectrum disorders?**

a. Difficulty focusing and maintaining attention
b. Difficulty understanding and using social cues
c. Difficulty with motor control and coordination
d. Difficulty with adhering to consistent routines

**37. What do nutrition experts recommend to most people for healthy eating and weight control?**

a. Multitasking, i.e., eating while working, driving, etc., aids in losing weight.
b. The kinds of foods people eat are what matter rather than the amounts.
c. When trying to lose weight, people should weigh themselves every day.
d. Most people need to change their lifestyles for permanent weight loss.

**38. Which of these is correct regarding what students must do to qualify for a career in FCS?**

a. The minimum degree required for employment in the field of FCS is the master's degree.
b. Students must participate in internship programs during 4-year, but not 2-year, programs.
c. Additional education courses and practice teaching are required for teaching certification.
d. Graduate work is needed to teach college, do research, or supervise, but not other jobs.

**39. The impact on a child's development of local communities belongs in which of the systems in Bronfenbrenner's ecological systems theory?**

a. The chronosystem
b. The microsystem
c. The mesosystem
d. The exosystem

**40. The proper decision-making process begins by:**

a. Defining the decision to be made
b. Listing the potential options
c. Researching potential solutions
d. Assembling a team to solve the problem

**41. Which of the following more accurately reflects what Bandura believed in developing his social learning theory?**

a. The environment an individual is in causes his or her behavior.
b. Environment, behavior, and psychological processes interact.
c. The behavior of an individual creates his or her environment.
d. Psychological processes cause the environment and behavior.

**42. Piaget viewed child development in social and moral contexts as a progression from**

a. Anomy to heteronomy to autonomy.
b. Heteronomy to autonomy to anomy.
c. Autonomy to anomy to heteronomy.
d. Heteronomy to anomy to autonomy.

**43. Of the following, which is an advantage of the demonstration method of teaching?**

a. Students can become more passive and dependent.
b. Students can learn best when the classes are smaller.
c. Students can develop observation skills and curiosity.
d. Students can learn but the method takes much time.

**44. What is the name of the economic condition caused by insufficient resources resulting in supply levels significantly lower than demand?**

a. Recession
b. Market failure
c. Stagnation
d. Scarcity

**45. Which of the following is considered to be the most important determinant of human comfort in housing?**

a. Relative humidity
b. Mean radiant temperature
c. Air temperature
d. Air quality

**46. What information is true regarding the law for Nutrition Facts panels on food packaging to include?**

a. Serving size, number of servings, and calories per serving are required.
b. Amounts of protein, carbohydrates, and fats per serving are required.
c. Fiber, sodium, vitamins, and minerals are not necessary.
d. All of above are true statements.

**47. Which of the following is true about people's nutritional requirements?**

a. Drinking tea or coffee does not affect a person's nutritional requirements.
b. Individual requirements for vitamin D are not affected by where one lives.
c. People who exercise more need more food, but they may metabolize it better.
d. Malnutrition is only found to be a problem in today's developing countries.

**48. When working parents look for services to care for their children, which of these is accurate?**

a. Many caregivers are charging lower rates than they have in the past to remain competitive.
b. Grandparent childcare is less common with fewer extended families cohabiting.
c. To be competitive, "hybrid" providers offer parents additional services included.
d. Au pairs' wages are a bigger challenge than associated government regulations.

**49. The values of nutrients on food and supplement labels developed by the FDA are currently called:**

a. RDAs
b. DVs
c. AIs
d. ULs

**50. As two separate ways of improving decision-making in management, what is a major difference between devil's advocacy and dialectic inquiry?**

a. Alternative reassessments
b. The number of alternatives
c. Acceptance of alternatives
d. Effects of greater diversity

**51. Which of the following scenarios demonstrates the use of joint decision-making skills in a relationship?**

a. Joan has decided that she and her boyfriend are ready to have sex, so she purchases condoms.
b. Tom purchases his wife Claire an expensive necklace from their shared bank account.
c. Rachel and Ryan decide to cut back on dining out to save for a home.
d. Carl considers his girlfriend's work schedule before deciding to plan a vacation for them.

**52. According to Kohlberg's theory of gender identity development, which of these is true?**

a. By 3–4 years, most children see similarities as well as body differences in genders.
b. By 6–7 years, most children see gender as stable but still believe it can be changed.
c. Children realize by 3–4 years that gender identity in most individuals is permanent.
d. Preschoolers label genders, but they do not comprehend that gender remains constant.

**53. In describing stages of child development, which ages did Arnold Gesell characterize as periods of equilibrium, consolidation, and smoothness?**

a. 2.5, 5.5 to 6, and 11 years
b. 2, 5, 10, and 16 years
c. 3.5, 7, and 13 years
d. 4, 8, and 14 years

**54. Some researchers investigating how teachers of Family and Consumer Sciences have been adopting technology in their instructional practices have found which of the following factors most influential?**

a. The ages of teachers
b. Technology availability
c. Anxiety about technology
d. Technology integration barriers

**55. Erikson's psychosocial developmental stage of Ego Integrity vs. Despair corresponds to which of Duvall's stages of family development?**

a. Stage VIII: Aging Families
b. Stage VII: Middle-Aged Families
c. Stage VI: Families as Launching Centers
d. Stage IV: Families with School-Age Children

**56. What should students taking occupational family and consumer sciences courses mainly be learning?**

a. How to prepare themselves for becoming homeowners
b. How to prepare themselves for careers on a lifelong basis
c. How to prepare themselves for getting paid employment
d. How to prepare themselves for balancing family and work

**57. In order to reduce the risk of spina bifida in infants, food manufacturers have begun adding:**

a. Calcium
b. Folic acid
c. Iron
d. Vitamin K

**58. Which of the following was NOT one of the consumer rights asserted by Presidents Kennedy and Nixon during the 1960s?**

a. Right to a safe product
b. Right to affordability
c. Right to redress
d. Right to be heard

**59. If large equipment has legs, the legs should provide a minimum clearance of at least:**

a. 2 inches.
b. 4 inches.
c. 6 inches.
d. 8 inches.

**60. Which of these did Albert Bandura discover in studying the influence of media on children?**

a. Young children's behavior is unaffected because they cannot tell reality from fantasy.
b. Children imitate violent behaviors, but not altruistic behaviors when they view these.
c. Children who viewed violent video material displayed increased aggressive behaviors.
d. Children who viewed violent video material displayed fearfulness but not aggression.

**61. Under the AAFCS's Code of Ethics, its Statement of Principles of Professional Practice includes that members eschew practices that exploit, intimidate, or harm others and that they maintain their profession's credibility. In which category of principles are these found?**

a. Integrity
b. Confidentiality
c. Conflict of Interest
d. Professional Competence

**62. Which of the following garments would be the most resistant to wrinkles?**

a. Rayon jacket
b. Cotton t-shirt
c. Silk shirt
d. Wool pants

**63. When giving advice, which example is the recipient most likely to hear instead of perceiving it as unsolicited, unwanted, and coercive?**

a. "You may find that easier to do if you try doing this."
b. "You must do it this way or it's never going to work."
c. "There is only one way to do that right and this is it."
d. "That's not working because you're doing it wrong."

**64. Relative to prioritization for time management, what does the "80/20 Rule" mean?**

a. 80% of the people in any workplace contribute 20% of the effort.
b. 80% of what we do contributes less than 20% to our work's value.
c. The formula for work success is 80% perspiration, 20% inspiration.
d. In typical workplaces, 80% of time is well used and 20% is wasted.

**65. Whereas Freud focused on male development in proposing the concept of the Oedipal conflict, neo-Freudians expanded on his theory to include the Elektra conflict for girls. In the latter, what must a girl do to resolve this conflict and thereafter have successful interpersonal relationships?**

a. Nothing; they just grow out of it
b. Symbolically "kill" their mothers
c. Want to be just like their fathers
d. Want to be just like the mothers

**66. For students preparing for careers in FCS, where do food manufacturers have jobs open?**

a. Only in product development and marketing
b. Consumer affairs, public policy, and research
c. They need FCS graduates in all of these areas.
d. They have no jobs open in strategic planning.

**67. When planning a menu, which should be decided upon first?**

a. What the entrée of the meal will be
b. What the side dishes of the meal will be
c. What the décor for the meal will be
d. What to prepare with foods bought

**68. Among the following, which is an example of a consumer right?**

a. Minimizing environmental impacts through purchasing choices
b. Following safety instructions to ensure the safe use of products
c. Sustainable consumption that will not impinge on others' needs
d. Accessing information that supports better purchasing decisions

**69. In some models of family life stages, which task is most typical of the "later family life" stage?**

a. Helping children develop peer relationships
b. Assuming the care for one's family of origin
c. Reminiscing and integrating life experiences
d. Coping with deaths in one's family of origin

**70. According to Murray Bowen's Family Systems Theory, which type of person has poor differentiation of self, depends on acceptance and approval, and is threatened by disagreement?**

a. "Chameleons" who conform to please others
b. Bullies who pressure others to conform/agree
c. This describes neither chameleons nor bullies.
d. Both chameleons and bullies fit the description.

**71. Which of the following includes the consumer's right to a healthy environment?**

a. The Consumer Product Safety Commission
b. The UN Consumer Protection Guidelines
c. The Underwriters' Laboratories
d. The Bureau of Competition

**72. Among the eight main goals of planning a menu, which two are reflected in considering whether there will be leftovers that can be reused, and whether the meal smells and tastes good?**

a. Presentation and meal service
b. Managing time and nutrition
c. Satiety and food practicality
d. Economics and palatability

**73. According to Piaget's developmental theory, when do children show the first signs of symbolic function?**

a. During the sensorimotor stage
b. During the preoperational stage
c. In the concrete operations stage
d. In the formal operations stage

**74. Which one of the following regulatory agencies is responsible for grading grains, fruits, vegetables, meat, poultry, eggs, and dairy products?**

a. OSHA.
b. FDA
c. CDC.
d. USDA.

**75. Which of these vitamins build up to harmful levels in the body if too many are ingested?**

a. Vitamins C and D
b. Vitamins A, D, E, K
c. Vitamin B complex
d. Vitamins never do

**76. For an FCS graduate who wants a career in marketing consumer products and services, which of the following represents one of the job descriptions she may perform?**

a. Giving personal nutrition, parenting, and financial counseling services
b. Conducting market surveys to discover consumer habits and interests
c. Bettering the design of consumer products or services in laboratories
d. Implementing plans for the marketing of consumer goods or services

**77. In which layout pattern are spaces arranged along a linear path, with major elements at either end?**

a. Radial layout
b. Dumbbell layout
c. Clustered layout
d. Doughnut layout

**78. When considering conflict management and resolution, what is true?**

a. Conflict in a relationship is a sign the relationship is unhealthy.
b. Because they find it unpleasant, people should avoid conflict.
c. Healthy relationships normally and integrally include conflicts.
d. People should avoid confrontation as they find it threatening.

**79. The four steps to the nutrition care process include assessment, diagnosis, intervention, and:**

a. documentation.
b. monitoring/evaluation.
c. problem identification.
d. implementation.

**80. Which of the following is a division of the AAFCS?**

a. The National Association of Teachers of Family and Consumer Sciences (NATFACS)
b. None of these is a division of the American Association of Family and Consumer Sciences.
c. The National Association of Teacher Educators of Family and Consumer Sciences (NATEFACS)
d. The National Association of State Administrators of Family and Consumer Sciences (NASAFACS)

**81. In researching elder-care services online, which website helps consumers find their local Area Agency on Aging (AAA)?**

a. Medicare website: http://medicare.gov/
b. LeadingAge (IAHSA) website: http://www.leadingage.org/
c. Eldercare Locator website: http://eldercare.acl.gov/
d. Argentum website: http://www.argentum.org

**82. What is the Betty Lamp?**

a. A modern lighting innovation that was invented by an AAFCS member
b. A kitchen appliance named after the founder of the AAFCS
c. A special project developed by the AAFCS to encourage household enlightenment
d. A colonial lighting appliance that is now the symbol of the AAFCS

**83. The daily values listed on food packaging assume that**

a. the food will be shared between two people.
b. the food will not be cooked.
c. a person's daily diet consists of two thousand calories.
d. the product contains preservatives.

**84. If a hospital foodservice orders food for its own production and produces, distributes, and serves the food all on the hospital premises, the food production system that the foodservice is using is:**

a. ready-prepared.
b. commissary.
c. assembly.
d. conventional.

**85. Which one of these actions is NOT included in consumer protection laws?**

a. Checking an organization's reputation
b. Enforcing antitrust regulations
c. Regulating bill collectors
d. Preventing sellers from fraudulent tactics

**86. How has the United Nations been involved in studying and dispelling worldwide gender stereotypes?**

a. The United Nations has not been directly involved with addressing gender stereotypes.
b. Through such groups and actions as an entity for gender equality and panel discussions
c. Only through advisory and technical services that further role models and best practices
d. It has undertaken to examine the impacts of gender stereotypes but not address them.

**87. In the demonstration method of instruction, which of the following steps comes last?**

a. Conclusion
b. Evaluation
c. Introduction
d. Development

**88. In household management, which of the following would be the first step to take in the process of solving a problem?**

a. To identify alternatives among actions
b. To predict outcomes of various actions
c. To collect data concerning the problem
d. To identify what the problem actually is

**89. Which kind of oil is NOT an unsaturated fat?**

a. Corn oil
b. Olive oil
c. Canola oil
d. Palm oil

**90. Which of the following equipment should be cleaned weekly?**

a. Freezer.
b. Food carts.
c. Ice machine.
d. Grease traps.

**91. In the Nutrition Facts panels on food packages, how is the amount of calcium represented?**

a. In the number of milligrams and as percent serving size
b. In number of micrograms and as percent Daily Value
c. As percent of serving size and as percent Daily Value
d. As percent of Daily Value and the number of milligrams

*Refer to the following for question 92:*

Jessica has decided to purchase a new house for $200,000. She goes to her bank to discuss her mortgage loan options. After selecting one, the loan manager processes her loan and hands her a document that outlines all of the details of the loan, including the interest rate, the total amount financed, any finance charges incurred, and the total amount she will pay after interest.

**92. Which of the following would have the lowest monthly payment for Jessica?**

a. A 30-year fixed rate mortgage at 6%
b. A 15-year fixed rate mortgage at 7%
c. A 30-year fixed rate mortgage at 12%
d. A 15-year fixed rate mortgage at 12%

**93. In which stage of family development do activities shared by spouses typically decrease dramatically?**

a. The expanding years
b. The developing years
c. The launching years
d. The middle years

**94. The synthetic woodwork finish that creates the most durable surface is:**

a. Lacquer
b. Polyurethane
c. Varnish
d. Polyester

**95. In her work identifying parenting styles, Diana Baumrind defined four dimensions of interactions between parents and children. Which of these dimensions is most related to parental tendencies to reason with their children to elicit the behaviors they want?**

a. Nurturance
b. Parental control
c. Clarity of communication
d. Maturity demands

**96. The child who assumes the role of the family artist, rebel, peacemaker, troublemaker, clown, or negotiator is most often which child in birth order?**

a. The firstborn child
b. The middle child
c. The second child
d. The only child

**97. According to the FDA Food Code, the most important step that foodservice employees can take to protect food is:**

a. wearing appropriate clothing.
b. handwashing.
c. restraining hair.
d. staying in good health.

**98. The primary advantage to participation in a group purchasing organization is:**

a. networking.
b. time savings.
c. accessing vendors otherwise not available.
d. cost savings.

**99. The sixth stage of Erik Erikson's psychosocial development theory occurs during young adulthood (i.e., between ages 18 and 40). Which of the following represents the developmental task a person experiences during this life stage?**

a. A person develops intimate relationships outside of the family.
b. A person creates or nurtures things that will outlast himself or herself.
c. A person grows more confident performing work independently.
d. A person establishes an identity separate from their relatives.

**100. In the developmental tasks he identified for different age groups across the life span, which of the following did Robert Havighurst include as a task during middle age?**

a. Adopting civic responsibilities
b. Adjusting to physical changes
c. Meeting social/civic obligation
d. Socially responsible behaviors

# Answer Key and Explanations for Test #2

**1. B:** According to some family life stage models (cf. Carter & McGoldrick, 1999; Carr, 2006), the stage of "family of origin experiences" involves primary developmental tasks of maintaining relationships with parents, siblings, and peers; completing one's education; and establishing foundations for a model of family life, which children rely on as adults to form their own families. The second stage is leaving the home (A), with primary tasks of differentiation of self from family; establishing adult-to-adult relationships with parents; forming intimate relationships with peers; starting to work, developing a work identity, and becoming financially independent. The third stage is the "premarriage stage" (D), with primary tasks of choosing a life partner; developing the couple's relationship; and deciding to create a home with the partner. The fourth stage is the "childless couple stage" (C), with primary tasks of learning, emotionally and practically, to live with a partner; and adjusting family of origin relationships to include the partner. (This model includes four more subsequent stages.)

**2. D:** While Tufts University is a reliable source for health information, the .biz domain indicates that it may not be a reliable site. University sites in the US generally use the .edu domain. Other domain endings do not necessarily indicate the information listed is false, but they should be validated using an additional trusted source. The .biz domain could be an indication that the site is an impersonation or commercial site.

**3. C:** Hepatitis B is not a reportable diagnosis according to the FDA Food Code, although hepatitis A is. Reportable diagnoses include norovirus, *Shigella* spp., STEC, typhoid fever (*Salmonella* Typhi) and *Salmonella* (nontyphoidal). A history of exposure to these pathogens (causing an outbreak or working in a setting with a confirmed outbreak) must also be reported by the person in charge. This person is also responsible for ensuring that the employee is appropriately restricted or excluded from work.

**4. D:** In interior design, the arrangement of elements in a pattern around some central point is known as radial balance. For instance, a dining room might be arranged such that all of the furniture extends out from a central table. The pattern of the radial elements can be based on size, color, or texture. Symmetrical balance is the arrangement of identical elements around a center point or line. This is the most rigidly balanced form of interior design. Gradation balance is the subtle but regular alteration of specific elements in an interior. For instance, a room might include various shades of the same color. Asymmetrical balance is the arrangement of unlike elements that nevertheless creates a balance when looked at as a whole. Harmonic balance is the agreement of the various design elements in a room. It does not entail any particular physical arrangement.

**5. C:** One component of CBT is breaking linkages or associations between eating/food and other activities, places, or experiences when those connections contribute to overeating, emotional eating, poor food choices, etc. Some techniques for breaking linkages include not eating in certain environments, not keeping poor food choices at home, finding alternatives to eating as coping mechanisms, obtaining social support, changing eating habits, and using positive reinforcement, problem-solving strategies, rehearsal, etc. Another component of CBT involves positive self-statements (A), which are used to replace self-defeating thoughts (e.g., "I'll never change," "This is too difficult," etc.). Evaluating readiness for change (B) is a component of CBT wherein the individual becomes aware of what he or she needs to do to attain his or her weight management goals and then commits to doing those things. Self-monitoring (D) is a component of CBT wherein one keeps track of things like food choices, portion sizes, and factors other than hunger that trigger eating. This increases eating self-awareness and supports focusing on long-term success.

**6. D:** Many consumers care about the way a car looks (A), and some are loyal to particular brands (B) out of their previous good experiences with it; some want a car that has a powerful engine and handles well (C). While these may all be valid considerations for customer satisfaction, what consumers should consider most is how they plan to use the car. For example, if their daily work commute and weekend leisure trips all heavily involve stop-and-go traffic, an automatic transmission is a better choice than a manual one. People who frequently drive on bumpy, unpaved roads or in hilly areas may need a vehicle with front-wheel or four-wheel drive. Those who regularly drive long distances and are on budgets need good gas mileage; people driving with many children and pets need spacious interiors, etc. Choosing a car to fit the individual driver's needs and purposes is thus the most important factor of the choices named.

**7. D:** When parents divorce, the family structure is necessarily changed; this is the most direct and obvious effect. However, it is very common for divorce also to change the family's income (B): One parent may have custody of all children but half the income of the couple or less. When couples split custody among several children, the parents' two households may have unequal incomes; divorce court-ordered child support and alimony may be less or more than the previous income of the couple; some parents fail to pay the ordered child support, etc. Community expectations (C) are also often affected: divorce can change where family members live, their types of homes, and where the children attend school. This in turn can cause neighborhood pressures on a family. All of these factors can change the family dynamics.

**8. D:** Women of childbearing ages need to replace iron depleted monthly by menstrual blood loss. Postmenopausal women no longer lose blood through menstruation; hence their iron requirements are lower. Vegetarians (A) often require more iron because their diets lack animal proteins that provide sources of heme iron. Young children (B) need more iron (in proportion to their body weight) because they are growing rapidly. Pregnant women (C) need more iron to support their babies' proper development. (Insufficient iron can lead to infant mortality, low birth weight, premature birth, infant health problems, and delays in infant motor and cognitive functioning.)

**9. A:** Bowlby defined a secure base as the parent or attachment figure who provides a constant source of security, functioning as the young child's "base," like a base camp or headquarters. Having this secure base enables the child to venture forth to explore the environment with the knowledge that he or she can still return to the base for security rather than lose his or her way. Bowlby defined the safe haven (B) as the child's being able to return to the parent to regain safety and comfort when he or she encounters a threat or feels fear. Bowlby defined separation distress (C) as the anxiety felt by young children when the parent is not there. He defined proximity maintenance (D) as the child's need to be near the parent, and in general the human being's desire to be near other people to whom he or she is attached.

**10. A:** The FTC was established by the administration of President Woodrow Wilson in 1914 through the FTC Act and the Clayton Act as the anti-trust legislation of the New Freedom. 1934 (B) was when the Securities and Exchange Commission (SEC) was established under the administration of President Franklin D. Roosevelt to regulate the stock market and securities industry; the SEC took over enforcement of the Securities Act from the FTC, which originally enforced it before SEC formation. Three of five initial SEC commissioners came from the FTC, one of whom later became SEC Chairman. 1979 (C) was when the FTC charged the American Medical Association (AMA) with anti-competitive practices by unlawfully limiting consumer information access on medical service availability and prices, restricting employment on the salary of doctors by hospitals and other facilities, and banning advertising. (The FTC's orders that the AMA revoke these restrictions were then upheld by court ruling.) 1995 (D) was when the FTC established its website, www.FTC.gov.

**11. A:** Since income tax must be paid, one should use after-tax income to determine how much is available to pay living expenses and debts for financial planning purposes. Using gross income before taxes (D) is unrealistic for paying bills, as part of that money goes to paying taxes. Taxpayers either have taxes withheld from their paychecks by their employers, pay estimated taxes in advance quarterly if self-employed, or pay their total tax for past year when filing their tax returns, etc. Living expenses and debts are NOT the same thing (B); they are two separate categories. Living expenses include mortgage or rent, utilities, food, health care, etc. Debts are accumulated amounts already owed rather than new monthly bills, like credit card debt, outstanding medical bills, loan repayment, etc. Assets listed *should* include savings (C), as these fit the definition of an asset, whether one plans to spend them or not.

**12. B:** Being able to analyze multiple features objectively, evaluate several different plans based on that analysis, and make a decision informed by the evaluation is an example of critical thinking, which is one of the areas whereby the FCCLA helps its members develop life skills. This example does not reflect the area of career preparation (A) because it does not involve learning job skills, identifying career interests, or making career choices. It does not reflect practical knowledge (C) as much as other examples such as knowing how to stay within a budget, drive a car, do laundry, cook a meal, etc. It does not reflect interpersonal communication (D), as the student's process of analysis, evaluation, and decision-making did not necessarily involve communicating with other persons.

**13. D:** Of the given fabrics, black satin would offer the best protection against sunlight. Dark clothing tends to protect the body from ultraviolet radiation better because they absorb rather than reflect the rays of the sun. Moreover, densely woven fabrics like satin have fewer holes through which sunlight can flow. Of course, black satin might not be the most comfortable fabric to wear in the sun. Dark clothing gets very hot, and sweating in satin clothing can be unpleasant. Many people prefer to wear cotton clothing because the looser weave allows for superior ventilation. However, most lightweight cotton fabrics offer little protection against UV rays, so it is important to wear sunscreen under the clothing.

**14. A:** An effective time management plan will encourage students to do the most difficult tasks first. This is considered by time management advisors to be the single most important aspect of successful time management, which is increasingly important in an age of information overload and nonstop distraction. This last point is the reason why answer choice B is incorrect: There is no way to eliminate every possible distraction. Instead, an effective time management plan should try to mitigate the damage of inevitable distractions. It is not necessary for a time management plan to be so comprehensive as to include meals, though some students may find it useful to do so. Making lists is the cornerstone of time management, as lists help students to prioritize their tasks and keep from feeling overwhelmed by the many things they have to do. Finally, because a time management plan will be tailored to the life of the individual, it will be different for each student.

**15. A:** To avoid cross contamination (the transfer of a pathogen from any item, such as a surface, tool, or item, to a food product), it is important to isolate raw foods from prepared/ready-to-eat foods. Foodservice workers must change gloves and wash their hands between preparation of different foods and must clean all food preparation surfaces between different food products. Different tools must be used to place raw meat and to remove or serve cooked meat. Foodservice staff must always wash their hands after handling trash or picking anything up off of the floor or from a contaminated surface.

**16. C:** An overconsumption of protein can put strain on the kidneys and liver. This is one reason why doctors discourage the use of body-building supplements and protein shakes unless under medical supervision. An excessive consumption of protein can lead to general imbalances in diet, which can undermine fitness in the long run. Protein does contribute to the development of muscle mass, but this is not necessarily a problem. Weight-lifting and vigorous physical activities require complex carbohydrates as well as proteins.

**17. D:** All of these choices reflect ways that young people can gain information on the career options available to them. Among them, the choice most likely to help them specifically identify their career interests, preferences, and goals is to participate in career assessments and in job-based exploration activities like visiting actual job sites and job shadowing (following specific employees and/or positions to learn what they do in their jobs). Career assessments help reveal the areas where students have the most aptitude and interest; and work-based exploration activities help students gain firsthand experience to identify which kinds of work they find most appealing.

**18. D:** Four expectations the NATEFCS work groups identified for beginning or pre-service FCS teachers were that they *should* be able to interpret standards, criteria, and processes for evaluating FCS programs and student learning (A); that they should collect data about program effectiveness and student learning outcomes using *varied* assessments, *including* performance assessments and authentic assessments, not only normed, standardized assessments (B); that they should not only engage in personal reflection and refer to evidence from various external sources, but moreover *should* adjust their teaching practices based on this information (C); and that they should use data-based evidence to justify their decisions about program design and teaching practices (D).

**19. C:** In his theory, Maslow proposed a progressive hierarchy of needs, often illustrated in a pyramid: He proposed each level of needs must be met before any higher level(s). The most basic needs essential to survival, which must be met first, are at the pyramid's base/bottom. Maslow termed these physiological needs, e.g., food, water, and sleep. As these come before all others, answer choice A is incorrect. At the pyramid's point/tip/top, Maslow placed "self-actualizing needs," i.e., to fulfill one's highest potentials. These can only be realized after all other needs lower on the pyramid are met; hence, answer choice B is incorrect. Maslow placed "security needs," i.e., for shelter and safety, second after physiological needs (C). Needing to feel love, affection, and belonging, i.e., what Maslow called "social needs" are third in his hierarchy; what he termed "esteem needs," i.e., to have self-esteem and feel personal worth, social recognition, and accomplishment are fourth. Hence, answer choice D is incorrect.

**20. B:** According to the AAFCS, its certification in Education Fundamentals can help recipients obtain employment and continuing education in both corporate businesses and nonprofits; in both public and private schools (A); in elementary, middle, secondary, and post-secondary or higher education (C); and in both schools and after-school programs (D).

**21. A:** The phrase "contains calcium to help build strong bones" states a mineral found in the product and what it does for the body. It does not make excess or exaggerated claims as to what the product or the calcium present in the product can do. The marketing phrases "nontoxic" and "all natural" are not regulated. These can be applied to products freely by the manufacturer. Personal testimonials and "satisfaction guaranteed" claims on products are an indicator of fraudulent claims, according to the FDA.

**22. B:** Intellectual disability is most characterized by learning in the same way as nondisabled peers, but at an overall slower rate. Typically, the autism spectrum (A) is more characterized by normal intelligence and learning at a normal rate but with deficits in specific areas, e.g., in social comprehension, range of interests and activities, and verbal communication for some. Sensory impairments (C) do not necessarily cause slower overall learning: deaf children take longer to learn reading specifically because of its strong auditory basis, but they learn language just as quickly provided sign language or other accessible modalities; blind children, given Braille or other methods, do too; and neither deaf nor blind children learn more slowly in other areas. While those with learning disabilities (D) may or may not take longer to learn certain things, they are not intellectually disabled; moreover, they do *not* learn the same way as others but learn differently in specific areas. They often succeed in these areas if taught differently.

**23. D:** Most white vegetables are low in vitamin A, including cauliflower (7 IU/0.5 cup), boiled cabbage (60 IU/0.5 cup), turnips (0 IU/0.5 cup), and rutabagas (1.5 IU/0.5 cup). Celery is moderately higher in vitamin A (226 IU/0.5 cup). Food that are high in vitamin A include bright-orange vegetables:

- Carrots (9094 IU/0.5 cup)
- Winter squash (793 IU/0.5 cup)
- Sweet potato (1444 IU/0.5 cup)

Dark-green vegetables are also high in vitamin A:

- Kale (8853 IU/0.5 cup)
- Romaine lettuce (2098 IU/1 cup)
- Brussels sprouts (1435 IU/1 cup)

**24. B:** Early childhood is a period of rapid bone growth, so young children need calcium in their diets. Nutritionists recommend serving young children 2-3 daily servings of dairy products and/or other foods high in calcium. Young children need adequate levels of magnesium and potassium, but these do not support rapid bone growth as directly as calcium. They do not generally need extra starches.

**25. A:** A consumer's credit score is directly influenced by the individual's payment history on car and home loans, credit cards, etc. While marital status, employment history, and income level may indirectly influence the credit score by affecting the consumer's ability to pay bills on time, of the options listed, only payment history itself is a direct factor in credit score calculations.

**26. B:** Research finds when consumers like the doctor they are seeing, they are less interested in considering price data for health care. However, when consumers have high out-of-pocket expenses (A) for health care, they are more interested in informing their decisions using price data. They are also more interested in the significance of price information when their medical conditions are not urgent (C) or serious because they have more time for health care comparison shopping. Consumers with few or no preconceptions about health care providers (D), e.g., through the influences of their own positive prior experiences, word-of-mouth communications, and/or advertising, are likewise more interested in using price data to inform their health care decisions.

**27. B:** The USDA recommends that in a healthy meal, the majority of food should consist of protein, dairy, fruits, and vegetables. Its recommendations for proteins and dairy are 1.2–1.6 grams of protein per kilogram of body weight per day. Most Americans eat enough protein; but the USDA advises eating a greater variety of proteins, and leaner ones. It recommends 3 servings of vegetables per day and 2 servings of fruit per day. Recommendations for grains vary based on calorie level, from 2–4 servings daily, but the USDA advises that the majority of grains we eat should be whole grains rather than refined grains.

**28. B:** Gender stereotypes are attitudes, but they often do attain legal status (A) when laws support them. For example, stereotypes of women as caregivers can prevent women from working outside home: Ireland's Constitution states its government should prevent mothers from having to "neglect" their household duties by assuring "economic necessity" does not require their outside "labour." While this law has good intentions to protect mothers from having to be both home managers and breadwinners, it can also limit mothers wanting to work outside the home from doing so. Thus, even laws with good intentions can also do harm (C). Stereotypes influencing laws often discriminate against women, but not only women (D). For example, the president of South Africa pardoned women with children under 12 years who were convicted of nonviolent crimes from prison sentences in 1997. A single father also with a child under age 12 and convicted of a nonviolent crime petitioned to declare this women's pardon unconstitutional based on sex discrimination, but the Court judged it nondiscriminatory.

**29. D:** When making a schedule, children should be encouraged to both include some free time and place the hardest tasks first. However, children should not be encouraged to block out long stretches to complete all homework because this would be too vague. One of the hallmarks of an effective schedule is specificity, so large categories like homework should be broken down into smaller tasks. At the least, the child should divide homework into subjects, and it may even be necessary to subdivide subjects into particular tasks. It is important, however, for a schedule to include some free time because interruptions and distractions are inevitable. If a schedule is too rigid, the student is likely to become discouraged when he or she is unable to meet it. Also, it is a good idea to place the hardest tasks first, as the student will have the highest energy and mental resources then.

**30. A:** The primary area of development disabled by cerebral palsy is that of motor skills. Cerebral palsy impairs control and coordination of the nerves and muscles in motor movements. Individuals with cerebral palsy do not have impaired cognitive development (B) unless they have some co-existing intellectual disability. Their emotional development (C) and social skills development (D) are also not impaired by the cerebral palsy itself (though they must have access to equal opportunities to develop these areas without such experiences being prevented by their physical disabilities).

**31. D:** According to Hall, high-context communication is an indirect style of verbal communication. It uses a softer voice (A) and relies more on nonverbal behaviors (B) to express meaning. In contrast, low-context communication is clearer and more direct (C) and spoken in a firmer voice.

**32. B:** The most accurate definition of opportunity cost is what you have to give up to get something else when they may be mutually exclusive financially. For example, someone may be able to attend school part-time while working full-time or work part-time while attending school full-time or to do each of these part-time, but they cannot do both full-time. Opportunity cost is not the reverse (A); it represents something lost rather than something gained. While it represents a trade-off, such an exchange is NOT always measurable as amounts of money (C). The cost can be lost time, lost enjoyment, or any other usable benefit(s) lost by choosing an alternative. Opportunity cost does NOT refer to the dollar price of a specific opportunity (D) like college tuition, a mortgage, a car's sticker price, the price for season tickets, etc.

**33. D:** It has been proven across multiple studies that individuals with higher socioeconomic status are more likely to wait until they are financially stable to marry and have children. Individuals with lower socioeconomic status are more likely to cohabitate and have children before marriage or to have children but not marry at all. Family environments impact the security an individual feels in a relationship. Personality traits play a role in developing healthy relationships by allowing an individual to find someone with traits that complement their own. Conflicting traits can lead to unhealthy or unsatisfying relationships. Tolerance in a relationship is a partner's willingness to understand or overlook that their partner has views or beliefs that vary from their own.

**34. A:** The sensorimotor stage is from birth to roughly age 2. The preoperational stage occurs from roughly ages 2-7. The concrete operational stage occurs from roughly ages 7-11. Infants to 8-year-olds are typically in one of these stages. The formal operational stage is around the age of 11 years and older. Answer D lists stages from Erikson's model, not Piaget's.

**35. B:** Satir identified five common roles adopted by family members instead of their true identities, especially when under stress. Always blaming, criticizing, and finding fault with the others (A) is one such dysfunctional role. Another is always trying to please the others (C) and apologizing. A third is always distracting the others (D) to deflect their attention from emotional concerns. Hence, none of these is considered healthy and effective because family members use these behaviors out of low self-esteem to conceal what they are feeling. (A fifth category she described is the "computer," who outwardly denies all emotion in favor of intellectualizing.) According to Satir, only those she called "levelers," i.e., family members who communicate their true feelings honestly, directly, and openly, are interacting in a healthy and effective manner.

**36. B:** A common characteristic in autism spectrum disorders is not understanding others' social cues, and hence also not using those cues to communicate socially. For example, an autistic individual might not understand that another person's smiling indicates happiness and/or friendliness, and may feel these emotions but not realize that smiling communicates them to others. Attentional deficits (A) are special needs more commonly associated with ADHD. Autistic people are more likely to focus intensely on one activity or subject for prolonged times. Motor control and coordination difficulties (C) are more common in developmental disabilities like cerebral palsy. (Autistic people may engage in odd-looking and/or repetitive movements, but this is not a motor difficulty.) Many autistic individuals adhere very rigidly to consistent routines rather than having difficulty with doing so (D); with autism, it is commonly a bigger problem if that routine is disrupted, which can cause "meltdowns"; or if someone wants to convince the autistic person to change a routine.

**37. D:** Nutrition experts advise people who want to lose weight permanently that they need to change their lifestyles rather than go on and off a diet, which results in regaining any weight lost. They also advise *against* eating while doing other things (A), which does not help in losing weight but more often leads to weight gain, as people are not mindful of what and how much they eat or when they are full. While some kinds of foods are better for us than others, portion sizes *do* matter (B). Some foods, e.g., leafy greens, can be eaten in larger quantities than others, e.g., ice cream; but moderation in the amounts we eat overall is best. Experts advise people trying to lose or maintain weight to weigh themselves weekly, not daily (C). Normal daily weight fluctuations from fluids and other factors make true weights unclear; weighing weekly makes it easier to know whether one has lost, gained, or maintained weight.

**38. C:** Students majoring in FCS who want to become teachers will need to take additional courses in education and also do practice teaching in order to obtain a teaching certificate. The minimum degrees required for employment in the FCS field are the associate's degree or the bachelor's degree, not the master's (A). FCS students are expected to participate in internship programs in *both* four-year and two-year curriculum programs (B). FCS students will need to pursue graduate education for careers in not only teaching college, doing research, and supervising, but *also* in food and nutrition, and in teaching at extensions and in other extension jobs (D).

**39. D:** What Bronfenbrenner named the exosystem represents the wider social system, including such factors as local communities, community resources available to the child's family, the work schedules of the child's parents, etc., that affect the child's development. The chronosystem (A) is what Bronfenbrenner called the temporal system that affects the child's environment, including processes and events like the child's physiological maturation, cognitive development, or parental deaths, divorces, and other experiences that alter development and life. The microsystem (B) is Bronfenbrenner's term for the interactions and relationships a child has with people in the family, neighborhood, school, and other environments. The mesosystem (C) is what Bronfenbrenner called the connection between parts of the microsystem, such as between parents and teachers, etc. (Bronfenbrenner also identified the macrosystem, meaning the system of beliefs, values, laws, customs, and other cultural influences on the child.)

**40. A:** The proper decision-making process begins by defining what decision needs to be made. Too often, students start working on potential solutions before the decision has been fully articulated. This leads to half-measures and ineffective decisions. Only after the decision has been outlined in its entirety should possible solutions be considered. It is a good idea to write down these options. Whenever possible, the emphasis should be on long-term solutions rather than quick fixes. In some cases, it may be determined that there is not enough information to make an informed decision. If this is the case, either information should be collected or, if this is impossible, the decision maker should figure out a strategy for mitigating this problem.

**41. B:** Traditional behaviorists believed that an individual's environment caused the individual's behaviors (A). Bandura proposed that not only do the individual's behaviors also cause the environment (C), which he called *reciprocal determinism;* i.e., the environment and the behaviors mutually determine one another, but moreover that the individual's psychological processes (D) also interact with environment and behavior to produce learning and shape the personality. Thus, he did not believe that any one of these factors caused any other(s) but that all three reciprocally interact and influence each other.

**42. A:** Piaget used the term anomy to mean that a child's social and moral development was not regulated, either by the self or by others. He used the term heteronomy to mean regulation of this development by others, and autonomy to mean regulation by the self. He characterized social and moral development in children as progressing from anomy (no regulation) to heteronomy (regulation by adults) to autonomy (self-regulation).

**43. C:** One advantage of the demonstration method of instruction is that watching the instructor actually perform a process, conduct an experiment, etc., both stimulates their curiosity to learn how things are done and also sharpens their skills of observation. Other advantages include that it is systematic; it wastes less in resources, effort, and time than when students experiment themselves; and it avoids the trial-and-error process students often undergo when doing it themselves. Disadvantages of this method include that students can become more passive by being observers than when they actively engage in hands-on learning and can become more dependent on the teacher to show them things (A); demonstrations work best with small classes (B), but many classes are so large they make demonstrations ineffective; though students learn from demonstrations, the teacher's instructions and actual demonstration are very time-consuming (D); and the teacher must have sufficient expertise for an effective demonstration.

**44. D:** Scarcity is the condition that exists when there are not enough resources to produce enough supply to meet the demand. This can result in an increase in price, as consumers are willing to pay a higher price when the availability is low. An example is when retailers increase prices on basic needs (such as bottled water) during times of crisis, such as during a major flood. Public utilities are unavailable, and people need drinking water. Some retailers will price gouge to profit from the scarcity of water supply.

**45. C:** Housing experts consider air temperature to be the most important determinant of human comfort. There are a number of factors that influence human comfort, but the primary concern for most people with regard to housing is to be kept warm and dry. In general, a house needs to be between 69 and 80 degrees Fahrenheit in order for its inhabitants to be comfortable. The other answer choices are other factors that affect comfort. Relative humidity is the moisture content of the air relative to the amount of moisture that could be in the air at that temperature without condensing. People tend to be comfortable in houses that maintain a relative humidity from 30 to 65%. Mean radiant temperature is the degree to which a person's temperature changes because of radiation. Depending on the air temperature and ventilation of a room, the people and objects within it will either absorb or give off heat. It is more comfortable to absorb heat than to lose it. Air quality is the amount of pollutants and noxious vapors in the atmosphere. Obviously, air quality correlates to comfort. Ventilation is the degree to which the air in a room circulates freely. The amount of ventilation appropriate for a room will depend on its intended use. Kitchens and bathrooms, for instance, tend to benefit from more ventilation.

**46. D:** Nutrition Facts panels on food packaging are required by law to include the serving size, number of servings per container, calories per serving; grams of protein, carbohydrates, fats, and fiber per serving; milligrams of sodium per serving; and the percentage per serving of the Daily Value for carbohydrates, fats, cholesterol, and also certain vitamins and minerals.

**47. C:** People who exercise more do need more calories from food since they burn more; however, exercise also enhances metabolic efficiency in some individuals. Drinking tea or coffee *does* affect nutritional requirements (A): both beverages interfere with the absorption of iron and zinc. Vitamin D requirements *are* affected by where one lives (B): people living in the northern half of the United States do not get enough vitamin D through exposure to sunlight during winter. People living closer to the equator have access to strong enough sunlight in winter for sufficient vitamin D, but they often lack exposure to sunlight during summers when they stay indoors with air-conditioning to avoid the heat. Malnutrition is a serious problem in developing countries today, but it is also an issue in developed countries (D) among people who eat too many overprocessed, refined foods whose nutrients have been removed.

**48. C:** To remain competitive in the current job market, many child caregivers are now offering multiple services, like housekeeping, tutoring, etc. Parents can thus get help in more areas for their money. However, due to inflation, many caregivers are charging *higher* rates, not lower (A). Another recent trend owing to economic factors is *more* parents getting help with childcare from their own parents (B). (Fewer extended families lived together in the recent past than historically, but this is changing.) Some families relocate to live with or nearer to their parents, and some invite their parents to live with or closer to them. This offers dual advantages of saving money on childcare and helping grandchildren and grandparents get better acquainted. Au pairs, i.e., foreign nationals, typically cost *less* in wages because parents provide their room and board as well, but State Department regulations limit their service, preventing longer-term provider continuity for young children. Hence, regulations are a bigger challenge than wages with au pairs, not vice versa (D).

**49. B:** Daily Values (DVs) are what the FDA currently uses on food and supplement labels to indicate the levels of nutrients in an average or standard serving of food related to approximately how much of each nutrient the average person needs. Recommended Dietary Allowances or RDAs (A) are what the FDA formerly used before the Dietary Supplement Health and Education Act

(DSHEA, 1994) required supplements to show Supplement Facts on their labels. Adequate Intakes or AIs (C) are amounts of vitamins and minerals included in the reports called Dietary Reference Intakes (DRIs) issued by the Institute of Medicine. These reports also set the Tolerable Upper Intake (UL) (D) levels for vitamins and minerals. DVs, RDAs, and AIs frequently have the same values, but not always. DVs are the only ones on food and supplement labels, so they are what consumers should consider.

**50. B:** In the devil's advocacy method, one alternative at a time is presented by the group, and one group member then critiques the alternative or the group's process for identifying alternatives by pointing out the drawbacks. In the dialectic inquiry method, two groups each select alternatives and each group then critiques the other group's choices. Managers listen to each group's presentation and critique of alternatives. Thus, the number of alternatives presented at a time is one with devil's advocacy and two with dialectic inquiry. With both methods, alternatives are reassessed (A) after being critiqued or debated. With both methods, an alternative may be accepted (C). With devil's advocacy, if not accepted, the alternative will be rejected or modified; with dialectic inquiry, if both alternatives are not accepted, only one may be modified and then accepted, or the two may be combined. With both methods, increasing group diversity has the same effect (D): a broader range of alternatives becomes available with more diverse members contributing.

**51. C:** Joint decision-making is a key component in relationships and requires communication between both parties. Rachel and Ryan worked together to decide on a life change for the betterment of their future. This is an example of joint decision-making in a relationship. In Joan's scenario, a joint decision was not made. While she made the decision to have safe sex, she did not speak with her boyfriend about it first. Tom did not consult Claire before making an expensive purchase with joint funds. Though Carl considered his girlfriend, he failed to consult her before making a decision.

**52. D:** Lawrence Kohlberg (who also proposed an important Piaget-based theory of moral development) found that while preschoolers aged around 3–4 years can label genders as boys or girls, they still do not understand that gender remains the same throughout life for the majority of people. He also found that at these ages, children have difficulty understanding that boys and girls not only have different physical characteristics but also share other traits in common (A). At ages around 4–6 years, children understand gender stability, but they still believe that gender can be changed by things like adopting the appearances and activities of the opposite sex. By around 6–7 years old—not as early as 3–4 years old (C)—they typically no longer believe this and realize gender is permanent in most individuals.

**53. B:** Gesell characterized the ages of 2 years, 5 years, 10 years, and 16 years as times when children's development is marked by balance (equilibrium), consolidation of abilities, and emotional smoothness or stability. He described the ages of 2.5, 5.5 to 6, and 11 years (A) as times when children's previous patterns are breaking up, resulting in disequilibrium and more difficult behaviors. Gesell characterized the ages of 3.5, 7, and 13 years (C) as times when children are internalizing and integrating things: 3.5-year-olds show unbalanced physical coordination and emotional insecurity, while 7-year-olds and 13-year-olds tend to rebel and/or withdraw. He described the ages of 4, 8, and 14 years (D) as periods when children's development is marked by "vigorous, expansive" movement toward the outside world.

**54. C:** In recent years some researchers studying how FCS teachers adopt technology in their instruction (e.g., cf. Redmann and Kotrlik, LSU) have investigated related variables, such as the teachers' ages (A); the availability of technology (B); teachers' technology anxiety (C); and barriers to integrating technology (D) like technology-to-student ratio, effective software for their courses, technical support, sufficient time to schedule technology use, and administrative support. Of these, teachers' anxiety about technology seems to have more impact on the variability of teachers' technology adoption than the others.

**55. A:** Erikson described people undergoing his stage of Ego Integrity vs. Despair in their old age, which corresponds to Duvall's eighth and last stage of Aging Families. Both feature adapting to the process of aging, conducting a life review, and preparing for death as tasks in common for adults. Duvall's Stages VII, Middle-Aged Families (B) and VI, Families as Launching Centers (C), correspond to Erikson's stage of Generativity vs. Stagnation. These share common tasks for adults of leaving legacies to children and grandchildren. Duvall's stage IV, Families with School-Age Children (D), corresponds most to Erikson's stage of Industry vs. Inferiority; both share common tasks for children of meeting new social and academic demands.

**56. C:** Occupational family and consumer sciences (FCS) courses are mainly for teaching students how to prepare themselves to seek and obtain paying employment, not necessarily for establishing lifelong careers (B). They are not for teaching students how to manage being homeowners (A) or for teaching them how to balance their future family and work lives (D). The focus of occupational FCS programs is to learn and apply FCS skills, knowledge, and attitudes that will help them secure paid jobs.

**57. B:** Food manufacturers now add folic acid to their products because it has been shown to reduce the risk of spinal bifida in infants. Folic acid is a B vitamin that aids in the DNA synthesis and cell production, and it is important in helping prevent neural tube defects. Pregnant women, women who are trying to become pregnant, and elderly people should all ensure that their diet includes foods with folic acid. There are also a number of safe supplements containing folic acid.

**58. B:** Presidents Kennedy and Nixon did not include the right to affordability among the consumer rights asserted during the 1960s. Businesses do not have any obligation to sell products at prices within reach of the average consumer. There were five essential consumer rights promulgated at that time: the right to a safe product; the right to redress; the right to be heard; the right to be informed; and the right to choose. The government enforces laws that require businesses to sell safe products or to clearly warn consumers about products that are not always safe. The right to redress enables consumers to receive a refund or compensation of some kind when a product does them harm. Consumers have a right to speak and be acknowledged by businesses. Consumers also have a right to as much information about products as they desire. Finally, consumers have a right to choose among a variety of products; it is with this in mind that the government enforces laws against monopoly.

**59. C:** If large equipment has legs, the legs should provide a minimum clearance of at least 6 inches so that it can be easily cleaned underneath with a mop. The same clearance is necessary for wall-mounted equipment. Otherwise, the equipment should be sealed flush with the floor so that nothing can go underneath it. Equipment that cannot be moved must be positioned to allow access for cleaning above, behind, and beside the equipment. Equipment that is mounted on wheels may have less clearance but should be moved for cleaning.

**60. C:** Bandura conducted landmark experiments wherein children watched video with violent behavioral content and found that the children did display an increase in aggressive behaviors after viewing, confirming Bandura's theory of observational learning. An additional concern with young children is that they often cannot distinguish reality from fantasy (A), but this does not mean their behavior is unaffected. It can more often mean they cannot understand or predict real outcomes; like that hitting others can hurt them. (For example, a child who sees a cartoon character blown up and then fine immediately thereafter might think this can happen in reality.) Children were found to imitate both aggressive and altruistic behaviors they observed (B). While some young children certainly reacted fearfully to video violence, the fact still remains that children did display more aggressive behaviors after viewing video violence (D) in Bandura's studies.

**61. A:** The AAFCS Code of Ethics' Statement of Principles of Professional Practice includes under the heading of Integrity that its members "avoid practices that harm, exploit, or intimidate others" and "endeavor to maintain the credibility of the profession by demonstrating integrity." Under Confidentiality (B), principles include protecting the confidential information of persons in their professional relationships and forming and sustaining trust, cooperation, respect, and confidentiality in professional relationships. Under Conflict of Interest (C), principles include members' actively avoiding conflicting roles and exploitation of people with whom they work and being responsible for treating others fairly and preventing, in fact or in appearance, divided loyalties. Under Professional Competence (D), principles include credentials, professional development, accurate representation and professional designation, competency claims, and practicing within the law and one's qualifications.

**62. D:** Of the given garments, a pair of wool pants would be the most resistant to wrinkles. Because of the thickness of the fiber and the general looseness of the weave, clothing made of wool tends to be very resistant to wrinkles. This is one reason why wool clothing is so useful for travel; it can be packed in a suitcase and not need to be ironed later. Silk and cotton products are moderately resistant to wrinkles. If packed properly, they can be worn without needing to be ironed. Rayon and linen are notoriously prone to wrinkles. Clothing made of these materials must be washed, dried, and stored properly.

**63. A:** This example suggests ("may," "if," "try") rather than insisting, as with "must" (B), "only one way to do that right" (C), or negating as in "doing it wrong" (D). Example (A) not only offers a mild suggestion, which the recipient is more likely to accept; it also frames the advice as being in the recipient's best interest. The other examples do not; instead, they give commands, implying that the speaker assumes power over the recipient. The recipient is more likely to reject or resist these as attempts at coercion. The form of communication in (A) is more likely to promote cooperation and prevent conflict; those in the other choices are more likely to promote defensiveness and/or conflict.

**64. B:** The 80/20 Rule means that 80% of our typical work activities contribute less than 20% to the value of the work we do. Therefore, if we only complete the 20% of our tasks that are most important, we still realize the majority of the value from our work. This rule is one of the primary reasons why prioritizing is an effective tool for time management. The other answer choices are NOT correct definitions of the 80/20 Rule.

**65. D:** Freud theorized that young boys unconsciously desired their mothers and wanted to get rid of their fathers as competition for the mother's attentions. He called this the Oedipal conflict after the Greek character who unknowingly killed his father and married his mother. While Freud omitted girls from this concept, neo-Freudians following him expanded it to include the Elektra conflict. Just as Freud said boys resolved the Oedipal conflict by wanting to be just like and emulating their fathers (C), neo-Freudians said girls resolved the Elektra conflict by wanting to be just like their mothers and imitating them. This is called "identification with the aggressor" because the child unconsciously fears retaliation by the same-sex parent for his or her aggressive impulses. Neither Freud nor the neo-Freudian psychologists believed girls just grow out of (A) the conflict. Symbolically "killing" the mother (B) is not how girls resolve the conflict; it is rather the impulse to do so that they resolve by identifying with the mother.

**66. C:** Currently, food manufacturers have positions they need to fill in product development, marketing (A), consumer affairs, public policy, research (B), and strategic planning (D). Graduates of FCS programs will be most qualified to fill these positions, so food manufacturing companies hope these graduates will apply for jobs in their industry.

**67. A:** When planning the menu for a meal, one should first decide what the entrée should be, as it is the "centerpiece" of the meal. The planner should then decide upon what side dishes (B) will go well with the entrée. The décor (C) should also be chosen to complement the entrée rather than vice versa. The menu should be planned first, and then the foods needed should be bought rather than buying foods first and then designing a menu to include those foods (D).

**68. D:** Having access to information that supports better purchasing decisions is an example of the consumer's right to education. Minimizing environmental impacts through purchasing choices (A) is an example of a consumer's *responsibility* to promote a healthy environment. An example of the consumer's *right* to a healthy environment is to reside and work in environments that are not detrimental to the consumer's health. Following safety instruction to ensure the safe use of products (B) is an example of a consumer's *responsibility* for safety. An example of a consumer's *right* to safety is to be protected against health hazards in products and services. Sustainable consumption that will not impinge on others' needs (C) is an example of a consumer's *responsibility* to meet basic needs. An example of a consumer's *right* to have basic needs met is to have access to shelter, water, and food.

**69. C:** The "later family life" stage is the last stage of some models (cf. Carter & McGoldrick, 1999; Carr, 2006), when family tasks include coping with physical deterioration in oneself and others and with losing spouses and peers; parents' relinquishing, and adult children's assuming, more responsibility to maintain families; and elder members' reminiscing, reviewing their lives, integrating their life experiences, and preparing for death. Helping children develop relationships with their peers (A) is a typical task of the "family with young children" stage. Assuming care for one's family of origin (B) is typically a task during the "family with adolescents" stage. Coping with deaths in one's family of origin (D) is typically a task involved in the stage of "launching children."

**70. D:** According to Bowen's Family Systems Theory, differentiation of self, determined by family relationships during childhood and adolescence, is important to intrapersonal and interpersonal health. Individuals with poor differentiation of self are overly interdependent with others and overly dependent on approval and acceptance from others. Individuals with poorly differentiated selves may be either chameleons, always changing their behaviors and attitudes to agree and conform with others, please them, and gain their approval (A), or bullies who pressure others to conform and agree with what they decide is right (B). Both types of extremes in behavior indicate poor differentiation of self; therefore it is incorrect that neither of them fits the description (C).

**71. B:** The United Nations Guidelines for Consumer Protections(1985) include the right of consumers to a healthy environment. The Consumer Product Safety Commission (A) sets product safety standards, as do the Underwriters' Laboratories (C). The Bureau of Competition (D) enforces antitrust laws and reviews business mergers to promote open and free markets.

**72. D:** Whether there will be leftovers that can be reused reflects the menu-planning goal of economics; whether the meal smells and tastes good reflects the goal of palatability. Presentation is reflected in atmosphere, table settings, etc.; meal service is reflected in choices like buffets, family service; Chinese, Russian, French, etc. (A). Time management is reflected in planning recipes that can be prepared and served in the time available (e.g., Is food ready when guests are hungry? Can the host sit and eat with guests, or is he or she busy with ongoing preparation and service most of the time they are eating?). Nutrition is reflected by whether courses or meal parts represent FDA food groups and proportions (B). Satiety is reflected in portion sizes, foods' nutrient content, and whether people feel satisfied after eating. Food practicality is reflected in whether foods in a menu are available; convenient to find, store, and prepare; whether guests like them; and whether any are restricted from guests' diets for medical, religious, or other reasons (C).

**73. A:** During the latest part of the sensorimotor stage, from around 18 to 24 months of age, Piaget said children develop early symbolic function when they begin using symbols to represent other things, like playing make-believe by pretending to be adults or fictional characters and using objects to represent other things or beings, for example, pretending a broom is a horse, a block is a phone, and so on. In the preoperational stage (B), children fully develop symbolic function and display more intuitive than logical thinking. Though capable of basic mental operations, they do not perform logical ones. In concrete operations (C), they begin performing logical mental operations but only concerning concrete objects or events. In formal operations (D), they begin performing mental operations that are abstract as well as logical.

**74. D:** The regulatory agency that is responsible for grading grains, fruits, vegetables, meat, poultry, eggs, and dairy products is the United States Department of Agriculture (USDA), which ensures that these products are properly processed and labeled. The USDA establishes zero tolerance for pathogens that lead to foodborne illnesses, including different strains of *Escherichia coli*. The USDA has a test-and-hold policy that requires that products be held until testing confirms their safety. The USDA maintains the Meat and Poultry Hotline.

**75. B:** Vitamins A, D, E, and K are fat-soluble vitamins, meaning they dissolve in lipids, i.e., fats. The body absorbs these vitamins in fat globules and stores them in the tissues. Therefore, if someone ingests excessive amounts of any of these vitamins, they can build up to harmful levels. Vitamin C (A) and the complex of B vitamins (C) are water-soluble vitamins, meaning they dissolve in water and are not stored in the tissues. Any excess amounts are excreted in urine and sweat. Because they are frequently filtered out, water-soluble vitamins do not typically build up in the body, but fat-soluble vitamins do. Therefore (D) is incorrect.

**76. A:** FCS graduates who choose careers in marketing consumer products and services may provide personal counseling in nutrition, parenting, financial management, and eldercare as well as doing or managing direct sales promotion, providing customer service in resorts, restaurants, hotels, and tourism or convention centers, or monitoring consumer trends, needs, and satisfaction. Conducting market surveys (B) is one job description among careers in research for FCS graduates. Improving product or service design in laboratories (C) is one job description among careers in product and service development for FCS graduates. Implementing plans for marketing consumer goods or services (D) is one job description among careers in operations management for FCS graduates.

**77. B:** In a dumbbell layout pattern, spaces are arranged along a linear path, with major elements at either end. This layout pattern is appropriate for houses or buildings in which there are two main places of activity, and it is a good idea to keep the areas separate. A radial layout consists of a number of paths extending out from a central point. This kind of arrangement is typical of offices and buildings with one central purpose. In a clustered layout, several spaces with similar size, shape, and function are grouped close together and linked along a central space or corridor. A doughnut layout, as exemplified by the Pentagon, consists of a circular corridor with rooms on either side. A centralized layout consists of secondary elements arranged around a central point or axis. One example of a centralized layout is a plaza, in which the central point may be a statue or fountain.

**78. C:** People cannot possibly agree about everything all the time. Therefore, in any relationship between or among people, conflict is inevitable, and it is normal and integral to a healthy relationship rather than a sign that the relationship is not healthy (A). Although people tend to find conflict unpleasant, this is not a good reason to avoid it (B). People also should not avoid confrontation just because they feel threatened by it (D). Conflicts provoking strong feelings are signs of deep personal needs that must be addressed. When people are willing to acknowledge their conflicting needs, examine them with compassion, and solve problems creatively, they can improve their relationships through managing conflict positively and respectfully, whereas avoiding conflict is more likely to damage relationships.

**79. B:** Monitoring/Evaluation. The four steps to the nutrition care process include:

1. Assessment: collect information through nutrition screening and nutrition assessment.
2. Diagnosis: define nutrition-related problems.
3. Intervention: develop a plan of care to address the nutrition-related problems based on data acquired through the assessment, and develop target outcomes.
4. Monitoring/Evaluation: assess measurable outcomes to determine if nutrition-related problems are resolved.

**80. B:** None of these organizations is a part of the AAFCS. All three of them are parts of the Association for Career and Technical Education (ACTE), the biggest national education association in America dedicated to preparing young and adult people for career success through advancing education. However, the AAFCS and ACTE are related in that the ACTE has a division devoted to family and consumer sciences, of which the other three answer choices are all sections.

**81. C:** The Eldercare Locator site helps consumers find their local Area Agency on Aging (AAA) and elder-care facilities in their local communities. Typing one's ZIP code or city and state into the designated box yields a list of local facilities or one may search by topic (e.g., Alzheimer's Disease, Caregivers, Elder Abuse Prevention, Financial Assistance, Food & Nutrition, Health Insurance, Home Repair and Modification, Transportation, Volunteerism, and others). Medicare's website (A) offers an overview of options for long-term care, a tool for comparing Medicare- and Medicaid-certified nursing homes, and more. The LeadingAge website (B) gives consumers information on what to look for when taking tours of prospective nursing homes. LeadingAge is part of the International Association of Homes and Services for the Aging (IAHSA). The Argentum website (D) also provides consumers with a checklist to use when visiting prospective nursing homes.

**82. D:** The Betty Lamp is not a modern lighting innovation (A). Rather, it was a lamp widely used during colonial times in early America, which gave a relatively good quality of light for the time. Because this lamp was historically used to light not only family life, but also all household industries, and because it could represent the enlightenment that the American Association of Family and Consumer Sciences (AAFCS) is dedicated to providing, the AAFCS adopted it as its official symbol in 1926.

**83. C:** The recommended daily values listed on food packaging assume a daily diet of two thousand calories. Adult males are generally advised to eat about this many calories every day. Women and children, however, may require fewer calories, while athletes may require more. When one's recommended caloric intake is considerably lower or higher than two thousand, one must make necessary adjustments to the daily values.

**84. D:** With the conventional food production system, the foodservice department orders food for its own production and produces, distributes, and serves the food all on the hospital premises. With the ready-prepared food production system, food is prepared in advance and then chilled or frozen to be reheated for service. With the commissary food production system, food is prepared in a central kitchen and is then transported to off-premises satellite locations for service. With assembly service, food is purchased already prepared and is maintained frozen or chilled until reheated for service. Many organizations use a combination of food production systems.

**85. A:** Consumer law topics include creating a fair marketplace by enforcing regulations, regulating bill collectors, preventing sellers from fraudulent or deceptive tactics, product liability, bill collector regulation, and utility shutoffs.

**86. B:** The United Nations has UN Women, the UN Entity for Gender Equality, and the Empowerment of Women. UN Women has held panel discussions, such as in Geneva (2011) on countering negative gender stereotypes and discrimination as part of its Economic and Social Council (ECOSOC)'s session. The UN also includes the Commission on the Status of Women (CSW). It states the UN General Assembly (UNGA), CSW, and ECOSOC "have been addressing this issue over time and need to continue to keep a vigil, and strengthen norms to change the cosmography of gender stereotyping." The UN's 2011 panel aimed not only to examine gender stereotyping's impact, but also to combat it and to identify "effective policies and norms" (D). The UN's advisory and technical services not only further role models and best practices, but also "implement, monitor and evaluate programmes," and these services are in addition to "advocacy, knowledge brokering, strategic partnerships including with CSOs, media and private sector" (C).

**87. B:** The steps in the demonstration method of instruction are in this sequence: First, the teacher introduces the topic or problem and what will be demonstrated (C). Second, the instructor demonstrates the process that he or she is teaching; this is the development (D). Third, the instructor completes the process being demonstrated, and class and teacher draw conclusions about it (A). Fourth, the teacher guides the students in evaluating (B) what was demonstrated and what they have discovered and learned from it, or the teacher evaluates what the students have learned by testing the knowledge they should have gained through observing the demonstration.

**88. D:** Problem-solving skills are among the critical thinking skills needed not only for academic activities but also in real life situations, including household management. Consumer and family sciences teach these. The first thing necessary to solve a problem is to identify what the problem is. Identifying different actions that could be taken (A), predicting what the results of those actions might be (B), and collecting information related to the problem (C) depend on, and cannot be done without, first defining the specific problem to be solved.

**89. D:** Palm oil is not an unsaturated fat. On the contrary, it is a saturated fat, meaning that excessive consumption of it can lead to heart disease. Coconut oil, butter, and lard are some of the other saturated fats. The other answer choices are unsaturated fats, which are better for the body. In fact, olive oil and canola oil can reduce the amount of cholesterol in the body.

**90. B:** Food carts should be cleaned weekly. Maintenance cleaning schedules are as follows:

| | | | |
|---|---|---|---|
| **Ceiling vents** | Monthly | **Garbage cans** | Weekly |
| **Cooler/Refrigerator** | Bimonthly | **Grease traps** | Every 2 months |
| **Dish racks** | Weekly | **HVAC system** | Every 6 months |
| **Dishwasher** | Weekly | **Hood filters** | Monthly |
| **Drain covers** | Monthly | **Ice machine** | Every 3 months |
| **Fans** | Monthly | **Steamer** | Weekly |
| **Food carts** | Weekly | **Walls** | Monthly |

| Freezer | Biannually |
|---|---|

**91. D:** Calcium is among several minerals and vitamins whose amounts are represented in Nutrition Facts as a percentage of the Daily Value (based on a 2,000-calorie per day diet). Calcium is also shown as the number of milligrams per serving. Calcium in supplements is commonly measured in milligrams, not in micrograms (B) as Vitamin D is measured. The amount is not shown as a percentage of a serving size (A and C) of the food, but as a percentage of the Daily Value (DV), i.e., the percentage of how much calcium is recommended in the daily diet.

**92. A:** A 30-year fixed rate mortgage at 6% would provide the lowest monthly payment on the $200,000 mortgage loan, because it has both the longest term (30 years) and the lowest interest rate (6%). This means that the consumer would be paying less interest on a yearly basis, and the total would be divided over the maximum number of monthly payments.

**93. A:** In stages of family development, the Parental stage consists of three parts: expanding, developing, and launching. When couples first marry, they share many activities. After they have children in the expanding years (A), the time they have to share activities as a couple is dramatically decreased. During the developing years (B) of the parental stage, children begin school: while families have limited time and more activities take place outside of the home, family members typically manage and share their duties successfully. In the launching years (C), children become independent, signaling the end of the parental stage of family development. After their children move out, "empty nest" parents return to being couples and having more time to share activities during their middle years (D).

**94. D:** Polyester is an industrial-quality synthetic woodwork finish that creates a durable surface. It is a heavy-duty finish that protects surfaces well from scratches and stains. Lacquer, polyurethane, and varnish are the other three popular woodwork finishes, but they are not typically as durable as polyester. Polyurethane is quite durable as well, but it can be difficult to repair when it is damaged. Varnish is usually easier to apply than lacquer.

**95. C:** The parenting dimension labeled by Baumrind as "clarity of communication" involves how wiling parents are to ask for their children's opinions and reason with them to encourage the behaviors they want as parts of communicating with their children. Nurturance (A) is what Baumrind named the dimension involving parents' protecting their children's physical and emotional welfare and expressing approval and warmth toward their children. Parental control (B) is Baumrind's label for the dimension wherein parents enforce rules for behavior with their children. Maturity demands (D) are what Baumrind described as the dimension of expectations parents have for their children to behave up to their abilities.

**96. C:** Researchers have observed that a family's second-born child may take on one of the roles named. A second child often feels he or she gets less attention than the first child and resents being compared to the older sibling. Some rebel against feeling bossed around by the older sibling as well as the parents. Firstborn children (A) are more likely to take on roles of "little parents" by being responsible, conservative, and high achievers. Middle children (B) tend to play very independent roles and feel relief at less pressure from parents, but they also experience less attention, appreciation, and family involvement. Only children (D) may interact better with adults than other children, but they are not known to assume the roles named as often as second children are.

**97. B:** According to the FDA Food Code, the most important step that foodservice employees can take to protect food is handwashing. Handwashing procedures require that, when using soap, the individual must rinse the hands of residue under running water, vigorously wash the hands for at least 15 seconds with soap, and then rinse the hands again under running water. The hands should be dried with disposable or single-use towels, and care should be taken to avoid touching door handles or other surfaces with bare hands.

**98. D:** The primary advantage to participation in a group purchasing organization is cost savings because lower costs are usually available to organizations that buy in bulk. Group purchasing organizations also usually provide additional services, such as verifying that vendors have an HACCP system, are in compliance with health and sanitation standards, and provide appropriate and timely delivery services such as in refrigerated trucks.

**99. A:** Young adults experience a conflict between intimacy and isolation in Erikson's sixth stage. During this stage, young adults begin to develop extrafamilial bonds. Success depends on a strong formation of identity that occurs in stage five. Failure to form relationships with others leads to isolation and loneliness, which can affect later stages: generativity vs. stagnation in stage seven and integrity vs. despair in stage eight.

**100. B:** Havighurst included in developmental tasks he defined of middle age (35 to 60 years) the need to adjust to the physiological changes that occur with aging. He included adopting civic responsibilities (A) as a developmental task of early adulthood (18 to 35 years). He included meeting social and civic obligations (C) as a developmental task of later life (60 years and older). He included developing socially responsible behaviors (D) as a developmental task of pre-adolescence and adolescence (12 to 18 years).